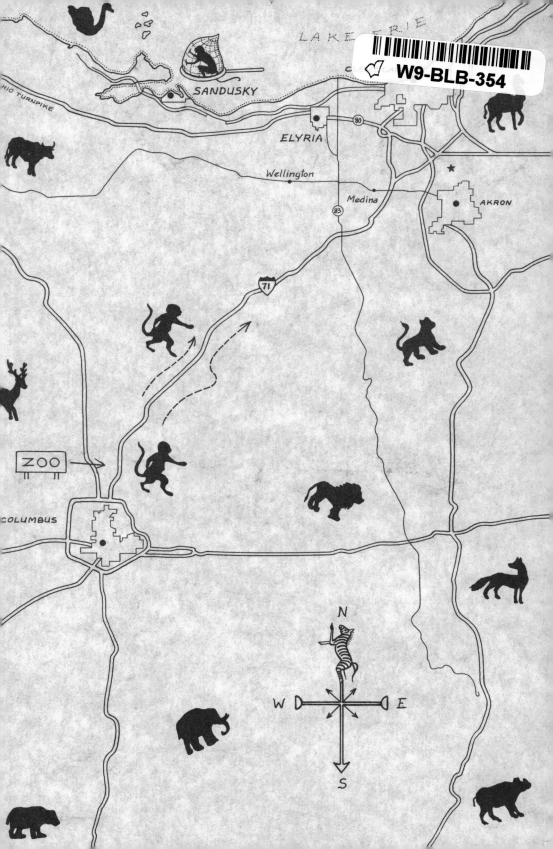

LAKE ERIE

W9-BLB-354

OHIO TURNPIKE

SANDUSKY

ELYRIA

90

Wellington

Medina

AKRON

83

71

ZOO

COLUMBUS

N

W   E

S

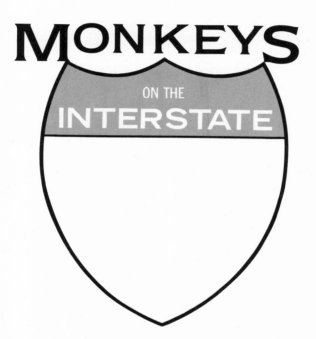

MONKEYS
ON THE
INTERSTATE

DOUBLEDAY
New York London Toronto Sydney Auckland

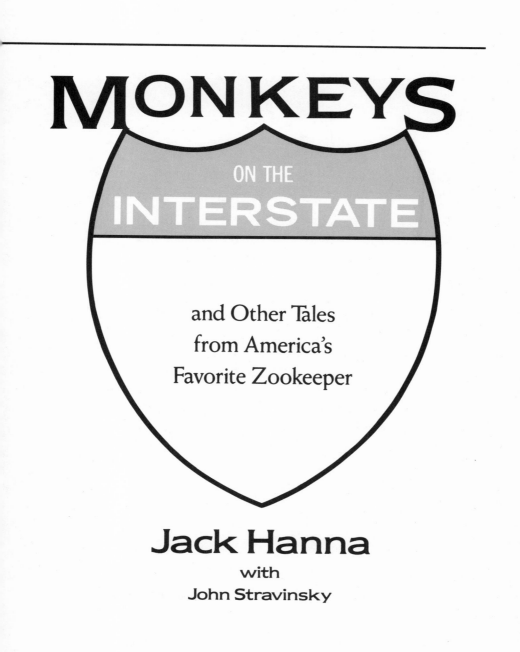

MONKEYS

ON THE

INTERSTATE

and Other Tales
from America's
Favorite Zookeeper

Jack Hanna

with

John Stravinsky

Published by Doubleday, a division of
Bantam Doubleday Dell Publishing Group, Inc.
666 Fifth Avenue, New York, New York 10103

Doubleday and the portrayal of an anchor with a dolphin
are trademarks of Doubleday, a division of
Bantam Doubleday Dell Publishing Group, Inc.

Library of Congress Cataloging-in-Publication Data

Hanna, Jack, 1947–
    Monkeys on the interstate : and other tales from America's favorite zookeeper /
by Jack Hanna with John Stravinsky.—1st ed.
        p.   cm.
    ISBN 0-385-24731-1
    1. Hanna, Jack, 1947–   . 2. Zoo animals. 3. Animals.
4. Animals. 5. Zoo keepers—United States—Biography.
I. Stravinsky, John. II. Title.
QL31.H29A3   1989
636.08'899—dc19   89-30574
                                                                    CIP

*This book is dedicated to my parents,
my daughters Kathaleen, Suzanne and Julie,
and especially to my wife, Suzi,
who has given so much care
to so many animals over the years.*

The staff of the Columbus Zoo. These great people make it all possible.
(Earl W. Smith III)

ACKNOWLEDGMENTS

To the Wolfe family, who founded the Columbus Zoo in 1927 and who have continued to support it ever since.

Many thanks to those individuals who brought me to the Columbus Zoo in 1978:

Jack Antrim, Dr. Joe Cross, Carl DeBloom, Mel Dodge, Dan Galbreath, Beverly Hagans, Jim McGuire, Don Nieman, Blaine Sickles and Bill Wolfe.

My sincere appreciation to those who assisted me with this endeavor:

Julie Estadt, Rick Prebeg, Nancy Staley, Sally Sickles, Vince Rakestraw, Mike Thomas, Buck Rinehart, Bob Shafer, Dave Tebay, Gary Robinson, Bob Shaw, Dan Friedman, Rosemary Mangieri, Ted Beattie, Doug Morris, Earl Smith, Joe Stegmayer, Jim Barney, George and Dorothy Egli.

I would also like to thank the staff of the Columbus Zoo, the Columbus Zoo Board of Trustees and the people of central Ohio, who have helped make the Columbus Zoo a beautiful home for so many species of animals. Without them, this book would not have been possible.

Thanks to David Gernert and the staff of Doubleday for believing some of these crazy stories; also, to all those who supplied the photographs so important to this book.

And a special thank-you to John Stravinsky, who hiked with me, flew with me, sat with me, jogged with me and spent many hours with many people to bring you this book.

A special tribute to Matthew Ramsbottom.

CONTENTS

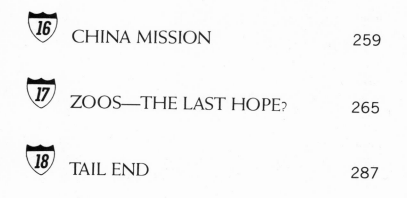

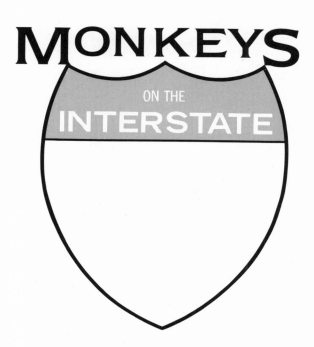

THERE IS NO ZOO

*T*hings happen to me. Sometimes I ask for it, sometimes I'm an innocent bystander. Sometimes it's funny, and sometimes it's not—at least when it's happening. Like when I was flying into Columbus, Ohio, in 1978 for an interview as director at what I understood to be the local zoo. Before I even landed, there was an air traffic controller trying to tell me Columbus didn't have a zoo. It wasn't funny! David Letterman does the same thing to me today, but he's trying to be funny.

I was too broke back then to buy an airplane ticket, so I had asked my good friend Stan Brock, co-star of TV's *Wild Kingdom*, to fly me up from Knoxville for the zoo interview—I'd pay for the gas. Stan is a hardy Englishman, an adventurer who will fly anywhere. Only a year earlier, we'd flown two jaguars down to the Amazon for release into the wild—but more on that later.

So here we were zipping over central Ohio on a perfect, clear spring day. Inside my new sport coat, I had my little letter from the trustees, my future employers. I learned later that they weren't sure I even owned a coat and tie. My being from Tennessee, they probably thought I had no shoes or socks either. From pictures, all they'd ever seen me in was safari clothes, which is about all I ever wear today.

Forty miles from Columbus, Stan asked if I'd like to see the zoo from the air. I said that'd be neat. He called the tower and said something British like "I say, old boy, could we vector over and have a look at your zoo from the air?"

The voice from the tower returned and requested a "repeat." Stan explained that he had a passenger visiting the zoo who wanted to see it from above. This time, the controller came back saying he had no idea what Stan was talking about, that Columbus didn't have a zoo.

Stan looked over at me and said, "Jack, old boy, what have you done this time?" We'd done some crazy things over the past few years. "Is this Columbus, Ohio, you want, or perhaps Columbus, Georgia?"

I said, "Stan, it's Columbus, Ohio—here, look at the stationery."

He told the controller that we had a letterhead that said Columbus Zoo, Riverside Drive, Columbus, Ohio. I yelled into the receiver that I knew it was north of downtown. About five minutes later, the controller was back: "Yes, we understand there is a zoo—up on the river. Just follow the river north of town."

We followed the river—luckily the right one—because there were two—and spotted the big dam, which was our landmark. I saw the zoo, and I thought, it's gorgeous, and it was, from the air. It was bigger than anything I'd ever worked with, the buildings looked neatly laid out, surrounded everywhere by trees, woods, and there was all that water—very few zoos are on water.

We circled it a few times, then headed back to the airport. I kept looking back at the zoo until I couldn't see it anymore. Did the place really need a new director? Was this the promised land?

After we landed and parked the plane, I went out front to get us a cab. We climbed into the back—I was still riding high from seeing the zoo—and the cabbie asked us where we wanted to go.

"Columbus Zoo!" I sang it out.

The cabbie turned around with one of those "don't mess with me" expressions, and for the second time in a half hour, I was told Columbus didn't have a zoo. He wasn't very polite, and I really didn't know what to do. I wasn't particularly thrilled with the lack of community interest going on around here, but at least *I* knew that there was a zoo, and we were damn well going to get there.

I shoved my letter at him over the front seat. He looked at it, unimpressed, and pointed out that the address was way to the north, which I knew already, and that he'd have to radio for a price on the fare. Now I'm thinking, uh-oh, big bucks, and I'm trying to save money. Stan just smiled and shook his head.

After over twenty miles of weaving our way up there, I finally saw firsthand that Columbus did indeed have a zoo, sort of. I hadn't really had a fantasy of what the place would

The Columbus Zoo, founded in 1927, is located on four hundred acres just north of Columbus, Ohio. (Rodger Schmidt)

look like, and I certainly didn't expect a grand physical plant along the lines of the Bronx or San Diego zoos, but I didn't expect what I saw either—especially not after the bird's-eye view.

The entrance, with its chain link fence, looked like something from a mental institution or a prison. It turned out they were working from a new master plan for the gate. (Everybody's always got a master plan to somewhere—half the time they never get there.) In front, there was a big mudhole, supposed to someday be a lake. Up close, the buildings looked pretty run-down, though I could tell right away that all they really needed was some fresh paint and a little stucco here and there.

What first struck me, especially on such a beautiful, sunny day, was that this zoo wasn't very crowded, to say the least. I also noticed right then that there wasn't much warmth around the employees, neither among themselves nor toward the public. Everybody was walking around like in one of those old *Twilight Zone* episodes. The animals that I saw were basically in sound, healthy shape, even if their environments were pretty ordinary. Aside from the pachyderm area, which had just been completed, there were no natural habitats. But with all this land, all this space, there was so much potential everywhere—so much to work with.

Something about the place quickly swung my mood back up. I guess it's something to do with—and I tell young people this all the time—starting at the bottom. It's like a new football coach coming to a team that's 0 and 10—you have nowhere to go but up. One major problem here was that the zoo was in the process of being booted out of the AAZPA (American Association of Zoological Parks and Aquariums). That's like a college team getting kicked out of the NCAA. You can still play, but who'll take you seriously?

Standing there looking at this 142 acres in partial disrepair, I had no idea, really, what the future would bring. I didn't even know if I'd get hired or not. But I knew immediately what the zoo needed, and how I could fit in. I wanted to put this place on the map. I wanted for every cabbie and air traffic controller in the state of Ohio to know about the Columbus Zoo—and how to get there.

I had no idea then about being on television, about saving people's pets (or people from their pets), about becoming a local celebrity—all of this and more would come with the job. I did know a few things about promotions and public relations, about community needs, about animals. I also knew that, for most of my life, animals and my love for them had carried me through.

In my ten-plus years in Columbus, it's people and animals together that have carried me this far. It's been a wacky ride, and hopefully the animal world and the people world of central Ohio are better off for it. At least today, most of them know how to find the zoo.

*O*ur farm in Knoxville, Tennessee, called Bu-Ja-Su after my brother Bush, my sister Sue and me, was the perfect place to grow up because there was room for lots of animals.
(Jack Hanna)

1

DOWN
ON
THE
FARM

Bu-Ja-Su, the farm in Tennessee my family moved to when I was five years old, was the kind of place every kid dreams about—streams, woods, horses, everything. My father bought the land after a successful career in real estate, and he named it after me and my brother and sister, Bush and Sue. It was so rural and isolated out there that it made the Knoxville subdivision we'd just come from seem like the inner city. It was here that I first became fascinated by little furry creatures.

We rode our horses up and down Ebenezer Road, a hilly rural route where we were the only inhabitants other than the chickens, goats, rabbits, pigs—you name it. Today it's a major highway. Bu-Ja-Su wasn't a working farm, but it sure was an animal farm—at least it grew to be one after I got going.

One of the first things I remember from Bu-Ja-Su was hand-milking a cow. There was an old mill up the road, one of the last of the old grain-grinding mills, run by a Swede named Ott Andersen. Ott had seven cows and he taught me how to milk them, a technique that, by the way, would come in handy thirty years later, when I would squirt David Letterman from a goat's udder on national TV.

Bush and I named those cows, and I loved them all—Kismo, Babyface and especially Streetwalker. We called her

Streetwalker because she was always busting out down the road. Today, zoo directors take clear-cut sides on the issue of naming their animals—it all falls under anthropomorphization, a long word and a sensitive subject in the zoo world. But kids will always want to name animals, and in that respect, I guess I'm still a kid.

I used to go to Ott's every afternoon and watch his mother make cottage cheese in little sacks out on the front porch. Ott made moonshine, too. Some days we could even smell his still up in the woods, but we knew it was illegal and were smart enough to keep quiet about it. Ott sold his booze to all the local farmers, but my dad wouldn't drink the stuff. He preferred Kentucky bourbon, which was brought in at night once a month. It was like in the movies. In fact, they filmed a moonshine movie, *Thunder Road*, right in front of our farm on Kingston Pike.

My first two pets were a couple of collies that were right out of *Lassie*. Lance and Vandy were big, beautiful outdoor dogs who went everywhere with me. One day, I went along with my dad to take the dogs to the vet in Knoxville. I'll never forget that day, because it was then that I met one of the most influential and important people in my life, Dr. Warren Roberts.

I was fascinated by every aspect of Dr. Roberts' work. I couldn't wait for his visits to the farm to treat our horses. Knowing also that he was the veterinarian for the Knoxville Zoo made his line of work seem as big-time to me as Mickey Mantle's job was to other kids.

At first I'd just go up there and hang around the Knoxville Animal Clinic and watch Dr. Roberts at work. I was probably more of a nuisance than anything else. Then one day, sometime during the summer when I was eleven, my dad went to Dr. Roberts and told him that I'd like to work for him. As a favor to my father, the vet said, "Okay, let's see how he likes it."

That first summer was for no pay, but that didn't bother me a bit. Dr. Roberts started me right off with cleaning

Me, Bush and Sue. (Jack Hanna)

cages. I'm talking dog crap—cleaning, scraping and hosing the cages of over forty dogs. Maybe I'm crazy, but I didn't mind it at all. I still wouldn't mind doing it today, and if I ever take a zookeeper's job someday—no problem.

Doing that kind of work, you really get to know if you like animals. If you can somehow enjoy cleaning out their cages, then you know you genuinely love animals.

I'll never forget the first time Dr. Roberts let me watch an operation. It was just a dog getting spayed, but there was blood and guts everywhere. I might have flinched at first, but mostly I just sat there and watched. I knew it was important, and I was mesmerized.

As I progressed, Dr. Roberts let me do more and more.

He was impressed with the fact that I wasn't too squeamish and didn't mind cleaning crap. Soon I was riding along in his station wagon to all the farms, and I felt like a big deal. One day up at a farm, Dr. Roberts handed me some rubber gloves, told me to put them on and "reach up into that cow and hook those chains around the calf's legs." I quickly learned not to eat my lunch before we went pulling calves, but there was no greater feeling than helping a creature come into the world. Again, I didn't earn a dime that whole summer.

There were no federal labor laws regarding children's summer work back then, and now as I think back, I find the situation today very depressing. You can't hire a fourteen- or fifteen-year-old youngster to do zoo work—I mean helping out and learning, of course. There are certain hours they're allowed to work, certain days they're allowed to work, and all types of insurance laws to cope with.

Work is work. My dad never questioned the nights I would come back from Dr. Roberts' office at ten o'clock. There was no lunch hour—I don't like that word. I would take ten or fifteen minutes to inhale the sandwich my mother had made me, then go back to working my little butt off. I'd polish doorknobs if there was nothing else to do.

The next summer, I asked if I could come back, and Dr. Roberts said fine. I was paid something like ten dollars every two weeks, and I never missed a day of work. If I couldn't find a ride, I'd take a bus or hitchhike the seventeen miles. I just didn't want to miss it, and I wanted to prove to Dr. Roberts that I could do the job.

Gradually, Dr. Roberts was giving me more and more responsibility. By the time I was thirteen, I was opening the business for him every day, cleaning, feeding and watering the animals before he got there. While doing this, I learned the value of taking care of animals. Like children, they need to be watched twenty-four hours a day, at least when they're at the vet's, or as I would later find out, when they're at the zoo. This sense of responsibility made me proud, especially when I'd be asked for my opinion, when Dr. Roberts might ask me something like "Jack, how do you think the Smiths' dog we operated on last week is doing?"

The most important thing to remember about animals in captivity—and the thing a child should be taught first about domestic pets—is that the animals are totally dependent on you. They can't feed, protect or even clean themselves adequately as they could in the wild.

I think one of the reasons Dr. Roberts liked having me around was that I kept him laughing. I provided a little humor as well as help. I always saw potential for humor in animals. I loved them, yet I was always telling stories about them—some of them I just made up. That's something I get flak over today. If I'm asked my "expert" opinion by some television host on what this or that exotic animal likes to eat, or when it sleeps, whatever, if I don't know the answer, I'll try to come as close as possible. I probably shouldn't do this, but I do.

The most thrilling days of all with Dr. Roberts were when we went to the Knoxville Zoo. That wasn't until my second and third summers there, and it opened up a whole new world to me. Sometimes we dropped by the zoo just on my account, even if there weren't any appointments for Dr. Roberts.

The star attraction of the Knoxville Zoo was Ol' Diamond, the largest African bull elephant in captivity. I was totally in awe of this animal—to me he looked like some sort of prehistoric monster. He'd come to the zoo from Ringling Brothers, who'd given him up when he became uncontrollable. Since then, he'd injured many keepers, just using his trunk as a battering ram. Everyone was afraid of him.

One visit I'll never forget was when Ol' Diamond needed treatment for a busted tusk. In the center of his corral made from railroad irons was a huge old oak stump that the elephant would spend hours sharpening his tusks on. One day Diamond got one caught in a crevice and couldn't pull it loose. He did manage to break it off, but it eventually became infected and needed treatment.

Treating any male elephant is difficult, since they're so dangerous, but it's even more so if they're ailing. Dr. Roberts tried to get up close to have a look—outside the bars, of course—and Ol' Diamond let him have it with a spray of spit that he blew through his trunk. From a safe distance, Dr. Roberts decided to hit him back with some antibiotic spray out of three-gallon containers. That tusk infection cleared up, but Diamond would eventually die many years later from a foot infection that couldn't be properly treated without risk to life and limb.

Most people have the wrong idea about elephants. Yes, they are intelligent and, yes, they can be friendly, but because of this, people are sometimes lulled into not taking enough precaution when dealing with them. They are the most powerful and dangerous of all wild animals in captivity and are responsible for more zookeeper deaths than any other animal. They can crush you in an instant.

Most captive elephants in zoos today are put through daily training routines that ensure safety for both animal and keeper. Several zoos have been attacked recently by wildlife groups for their elephant-training methods. (The controversy centers on a stick with a blunt metal hook— used in India for hundreds of years—that is used for directing the animal's attention and maintaining respect.) Although cruelty is never acceptable, keepers must be able to control these powerful animals; daily training routines establish and maintain their authority while allowing the animals to be treated.

Control and captive breeding of elephants could play an important part in their survival as a species. In the fall of 1988, 150 African elephants were illegally poached for ivory over a few months in Kenya alone. Only 11,000 elephants are left in Kenya, down from 140,000 in 1970.

I didn't know it at the time, but my working with Dr.

Roberts was laying the groundwork for some sort of animal-related career. Young people are always asking me what kind of degree to work toward in college, what kind of studies to focus on to get into my line of work. Well, there are only about 4,600 people employed today in the nationwide zoo community, from keepers to maintenance men to zoo directors. At approximately 150 zoos, there are but eighty or so major zoo directors. So it's a tight job market. Your studies and the field you major in are always important, but they won't get you into the zoo business. I'm not going to tell anyone not to study zoology, but what is important is to find out if you really like the work. Go clean up crap, whatever, on a farm, or at a zoo or veterinary clinic, get your hands dirty. Find out if you like working with animals and people, if you can stand long and odd hours. I did and I loved it and I still do.

All the time that I was working at Dr. Roberts' I was also building up my little menagerie out at Bu-Ja-Su. With my brother Bush and my sister Sue, we had pigs, goats, horses, rabbits, birds, just about anything we could handle that moved. I even had a big pet groundhog whom we stuffed when he died. Bush still has him. I'd go down to the creek and catch huge fish, then put them in the little ponds we had. Sometimes I kept them in the toilet bowl temporarily before transfer. Of course, my mother wasn't thrilled.

My parents were usually quite tolerant of all my animal whims. My father had grown up in rural, backwoods Arkansas, so he understood. My mother, being from a good northern city family in St. Paul, Minnesota, just shook her head most of the time.

With my rabbit collection, I pushed them both too far. It started out innocently enough with three females and two males, but, well, rabbits will be rabbits. They began to breed. I was fascinated with the little devils and was intent on seeing them multiply as fast as possible. I built forty rabbit hutches with runs and back doors, a whole intricate setup. I cleaned up after them all the time and loved it. My dad kept after me to give some away to friends or pet shops—or to his friends, who would eat them, but of course I wouldn't go for that. He even knew people who would buy them from me, or so he said. Finally when my rabbit family grew to over a hundred, he'd had enough. One day he told me he was going to have Lloyd, a man who worked on the farm, "dispose" of them. Well, no way was I going to let Lloyd kill my rabbits. So that night I went out and let every last one of those suckers loose on the farm, which really upset my father. Three, four years later you could still see white-and-brown rabbits crossing Ebenezer Road.

When I was fourteen, I received the Christmas gift that I'd been lobbying for for over a year: two miniature donkeys about the size of large sheepdogs. I had been crazy about these things ever since I'd read about them in some magazine. They were beautiful, from Sicily, with a little donkey cart and brand-new harnesses. It was the best Christmas I ever had.

Those donkeys bred and of course, before long, I was collecting the things. I bought two more off some other guy and all of a sudden I saw myself in the donkey business. It wasn't quite what my parents had in mind.

It would have been nice to say that I never spent enough time with my homework and that's why my grades were so bad, but I actually did work hard, I just wasn't very gifted when it came to books and studying. When I was fifteen, my poor marks were such an embarrassment to my family that my father decided to send me away to Kiski, a boarding school in Saltsburg, Pennsylvania (provided, of course, that they'd let me in). I was leaving Webb, a private day school that didn't want me back. My father took me to meet the Kiski headmaster, Mr. Jack Pidgeon, and everything went pretty smoothly, until I asked him if I could bring my donkeys to school. My father about went through the ceiling, but Mr. Pidgeon thought it was kind of funny. He told us that I could come, but that the donkeys would have to stay at home.

I missed my wildlife at Kiski—though I did try to work animals into school life in one way or another. I started a pig-greasing contest that turned into a big fund-raiser. We were the Kiski Cougars, and I tried to order a cougar for a mascot, but they weren't going to let us keep it, so I dropped that. A long time ago, the school's nickname was the Squirrels; I was always trying to trap squirrels for mascots, but I never got one. I continued to have trouble with my studies, but I worked harder than ever. Fortunately, they had "effort" grades and I did receive the proverbial "A's for effort."

One subject that I found to my liking was speech, and it's probably the most important subject I ever had. I've given hundreds of speeches over the last twenty years, but I'll never forget my first speech back at Webb. The subject was, surprise, rabbits, and I brought five or six of them with me. That's something I learned back then, and I've stuck to it ever since: always bring an animal (at least one) along to any public speaking appearance. The late Guy Smith, Director of the Knoxville Zoo, always had an animal with him when making speeches.

Here again is a bone of contention among zoo-world people: should some animals be taken out of their everyday environment and risk being stressed? I understand the dilemma, but I'm always very careful with the animals I select, and I firmly believe that we're doing more good by educating, showing these animals up close and getting people interested in them, than we are doing bad by taking them out of their zoo environment.

Anyway, here I was in front of the whole student body, two hundred boys, and I was showing how to hold a rabbit. I picked up the rabbit behind the neck and it peed and crapped all over my arm, just like what happens on Letterman these days. If I was embarrassed at first, I quickly caught on to the value of a few laughs while speaking in public. So that's where all that started.

After graduating from Kiski, I was somehow admitted to

Muskingum, a small liberal arts college in New Concord, Ohio. I say somehow because my SAT scores were terrible. However, the SAT scores would not keep me from serving on the board of trustees of both Kiski and Muskingum, which I am proud to do today. Actually, I talked my way into that school, and I knew enough this time not to tell them I would bring along a donkey, which, of course, I did. The donkey stayed behind the fraternity house until the authorities found out. Then I had to move it to a farm outside of town—which cost me thirty dollars a month. The donkey eventually became the school mascot and helped me meet the girl of my life, Suzi Egli.

Across the row from me in French class sat a pretty girl whom I always wanted to talk to. She was also well en-

My miniature donkey, Doc, wasn't allowed to go to prep school with me, but he did come to Muskingum College. He lived behind the fraternity house and became the official mascot for our teams. (*The Black and Magenta*, Muskingum College)

*S*uzi and Doc at a Muskingum football game.
(*The Black and Magenta,* Muskingum College)

dowed, and one day the buttons on her blouse were open and she was being laughed at by some football players. I wouldn't have minded looking myself, but the laughter bothered me. So I leaned over and told her that her "stomach" was showing.

With my unfashionable Coke-bottle glasses, my baggy pants and white socks, I wasn't much of a ladies' man. But Suzi, the girl in French class and captain of the cheerleading squad, somehow thought I was funny, and when she heard about my donkey, she thought I was a real character. I kept her going with my stories about my donkeys, and we quickly became fast friends. Later that year, we danced once, and it just took off from there.

If I've made it this far through all the animal craziness over the years, I have to thank Suzi for going along with everything all the way. The first year that I knew her, she took me to Long Island to go fishing for flounder with her father, who was then a minister and school principal from Wayne, New Jersey. One the way back, we stopped at a Long Island duck farm. I looked out over all those cute little penned-in ducks and asked Mr. Egli, "These are pet ducks, right?"

"No," he said, "these ducks are to eat."

I decided right then that three of them were going to be pets. I picked out three choice little ones, bought them and told Suzi and her father that I was taking them back to Muskingum.

"You're not really going to take those back to college, are you?" he asked me.

"Oh yes, he is," giggled Suzi. We named them Aquaduck, Viaduck and Ovaduck, and I took care of them all through college. When Suzi and I became engaged our junior year, we left those ducks in the college lake. Every year I give ducks and swans to Muskingum and I make sure they get to that lake.

We got married our senior year, much to the dismay of our parents, who thought it was too soon. Just before we hitched up in December, Dr. Bill Miller, president of Muskingum, called me into his office. I was scheduled to graduate a semester early, the week before our wedding.

When I entered his office, Dr. Miller was looking over a form on career choices that I'd filled out months earlier.

"It says here that you want to be a zoo director," he said, looking at me funny.

"That's right, sir."

"I didn't know anybody ever wanted to be a zoo director. This college is almost a hundred and fifty years old, I've been here thirty-seven years, and as far as I can recall, no one's ever put down 'zoo director.' You're sure about this?"

"Positive."

"Well, good luck with it."

I had no idea then how much I would need it.

*B*ush and I outside of Pet Kingdom with my lion, Daisy, and an African pygmy goat.
(John Gilbreath)

2

HANNA'S ARK— A GROWING MENAGERIE

After finishing college, Suzi and I moved back to Knoxville, where I began to collect a variety of exotic animals and where our first daughter, Kathaleen, was born. Maybe I was making up for lost time, but I'd always known that, once I was old enough, I could and would have all the pets or wild critters I wanted. I went full steam ahead with this idea, and it just about ruined us.

My father gave us a cottage on the farm to live in for several months, and the area was perfect for my grandiose plans. Suzi was always a great sport about it; in fact, her enthusiasm often matched mine. Some people spend money on clothes, diamonds, cars, what have you; our thing was animals—even if we didn't have the money. Ever heard of buying a chimpanzee on credit? Have monkey, pay later.

Like so many newlyweds just out of college, we had a rough first year. A number of odd jobs and small-time business ventures just never worked out. If they didn't involve animals, my heart wasn't in it.

I bought a chain saw and put an ad in the paper selling firewood. The first tree I cut down fell through somebody's greenhouse and caused $2,000 worth of damage. I tried to mow yards and ran over a man's vegetable garden. I invested in an all-terrain-vehicle scheme in which I had to buy the first one, a demo model. I couldn't earn a dime until I sold one, which I never did. During a demonstration next to a shopping mall, the thing overturned on a hill, resulting in a mess of stitches to my passenger. After being fortunate enough not to get sued, I quit that business while I was ahead.

At one point that year, I planned to turn Bu-Ja-Su into a zoo. An architect drew up the blueprints, and I even had a name: West Knoxville Zoo. In the beginning, I would just add animals I could afford; later I'd expand. My father was terrifically supportive. He even pleaded my case before the county commissioners, but zoning was denied. I still think it was a good idea, it could have been a great place for both people and animals.

Meanwhile, our zoo at home included lions, llamas, deer, buffaloes, elk, chimpanzees, a mynah bird, and other odd and assorted critters. Somehow, they all seemed to get along. It was helter-skelter, but it was a lot of fun. Some were in the house, some were outside in the yard, some were penned in. Seems like I was always building new pens and enclosures, putting up more fencing.

Most of my animals were purchased fairly cheap through mail-order catalogues, something you could never do today. Some of these catalogues were actually very sleazy and generally disregardful of species preservation, but at the time they were my bibles.

In the 1960s, you could order and have delivered to your home almost any kind of animal, no matter how endangered or how dangerous. You could buy pet raccoons, possibly carrying rabies, for $35, ocelots, which today are endangered, for $95, bears, mountain lions, timber wolves, deadly copperheads and cottonmouth moccasin snakes. How about a golden eagle for $75? Most zoos today would have difficulty even finding a golden eagle to put on exhibit. No questions were ever asked; it was cash business.

The animals were usually in good shape. The only problem was where they would go and who would buy

PRICE CATALOGUE

No. 63, Year 1961

Over 36 Years in this Business!

THE TRAILS END ZOO
ST. STEPHEN, SO. CAROLINA

MONKEYS -

	per each
	$627.50
Young Chimpanzees	117.50
Woolly Monkeys	47.50
Spider Monkeys	47.50
Ringtail Monkeys	57.50
Cupuchin Monkeys	37.50
Marmossets	37.50

Squirrel Monkeys $4.50

Box Tortoises & Turtles, postpaid .... 6 for $3.00
Chameleons, postpaid .... 2 for $2.50
Fence Swifts, postpaid $3.00
Red-Head Skinks, postpaid

SQUIRRELS -

So.eastern Fox Squirrels, illus. here .... $95.00 pr.
Chipmunks .... 15.00 pr.
Red Squirrels .... 25.00 pr.
Flying Squirrels .... 15.00 pr. .... 25.00 pr.

Grey Squirrels, $15.00 ea. or
We also have hand-raised
Pet Grey Squirrels, very
lovely .... $25.00 ea.

WILD ANIMALS -

	per each
Hand-raised	
Pet Raccoons	$35.00
Untamed	
Foxes	20.00
Opossums	17.50
Bob-Cats	7.50
Badgers	40.00
Armadillos	
Ferrets	10.00
Ocelots	15.00
Coatis-mundis	95.00
Elk. Bears	37.50
Mt. Lions	150.00
Kinkajous	225.00
Ringtail Cats	85.00
Coyotes	25.00
Ottars	37.50
	175.00

Kinkajou

This tiny little pamphlet was how I ordered some of my first animals.
(Jack Hanna)

them. Most people wouldn't have the faintest idea of the feeding or habitat needs of a bobcat, a red-tailed hawk, or a woolly monkey—all of which could be bought by mail. Fortunately, most of the animals available back then are protected today. But can you imagine sending someone a rattlesnake for Christmas? Until just a few years ago, you actually could.

My main animal dealer was a man named Bill Chase down in Miami, who got his animals from the wild or from breeders. He was an old-timer who sold to zoos and pet shops as well as to private individuals. I learned a great deal about animals from him. There were very few regulations then, but he always went to great lengths to ensure that his animals were in great shape, and they always were. Today there are international laws that regulate trade in exotic animals, but back then all a dealer needed was to place an order and wait.

The first animal I ever ordered from Chase was an African pygmy goat. I drove out to the Knoxville airport to pick it up with Suzi, and we brought the crate back home to open in front of my father. When he saw it, he was less excited than we were. He asked me what I paid for it. "Well, the airfare was three hundred dollars," I told him, "but the goat only cost seventy-five dollars."

"What?" my dad exploded. "You paid three hundred seventy-five dollars for a damn goat?" He couldn't believe it.

"Yeah, but this is a pygmy goat from Africa," I explained. "I'm going to make a lot of money with this goat."

"Looks like a regular goat to me," he said, and just walked away. I never made a penny with that goat.

Appropriately enough, my string of odd jobs ended with a six-week stint in a brand-new pet shop. The owner was a Mr. Rasmussen, a nice German man, who had absolutely no business sense at all. Mine wasn't much better, but I did help him start up his business in time for Christmas 1970. At the same time, I learned everything I could about pet shops: where to obtain dogs, cats, fishes, who all the wholesalers were, where to get all the paraphernalia, etc. One day I came home and told Suzi I was going to borrow some money and open up my own pet store.

The timing of this venture, Pet Kingdom, worked out perfectly, since my brother was in the process of buying an old motel and had some space to spare. I never could have done it without my father and my brother. It was one of those great inspired efforts: "Hey, let's build a pet store." And we did.

I'll never forget the excitement of opening day. We had about forty fish tanks, loads of boarding kennels for dogs and cats and, of course, some exotic animals, which were not for sale. Everything was meticulously clean, all the animals were healthy. I even had a little petting zoo out back with baby llamas, miniature donkeys, goats, ducks and other furry creatures.

Pet Kingdom was successful right off the bat, and it probably caused me to get a little carried away with my private zoo back at the farm. Probably the only time in my life that I ever remember my dad flat out saying "no" to one of my plans was when I tried to buy an elephant. That's right, an elephant. Ever since my days with Dr. Roberts, I loved elephants—working with them, reading about them, even cleaning up after them. My mistake was buying one without checking with my dad first, especially since it was going to live on his property.

In the winter of 1971, Suzi and I had gone down to Florida to visit my parents, who were vacationing. We took a little side trip over to Chase's in Miami and found the cutest little Indian bull elephant. I say little, it actually weighed about three hundred pounds and was still being bottle-fed. Today, such an animal is endangered and will cost about $40,000 on the zoo market. Anyway, we put a $500 deposit on this little guy—his name was Crumb— who cost $2,000 total. We went back to the farm—my parents were still out of town—and with my brother, began fixing up a cattle barn into an elephant house. We put

Kathaleen and I in Pet Kingdom's petting zoo with Alfred the llama.
(*Knoxville Journal*, Hugh Lunsford)

heating in, a concrete floor, big pilings, drains, the works.

When my dad came home, he of course wanted to know what the hell was going on in the barn.

"I bought a baby elephant," I told him. I was actually quite excited about telling him, even if I didn't know how he'd react.

"How much did you pay for him?" he asked.

"Two thousand dollars. Actually only five hundred dollars on deposit," I told him.

"You just lost five hundred dollars," he said.

Looking back on it, not buying that elephant was one of the better things that's ever happened to me. I wish I had been so lucky with Daisy, our lioness.

By the time our second daughter, Suzanne, was born, we had built our dream house, which we named Hanna's Ark. This was another family effort, aided by a seventy-two-year-old man named Mr. Ball. The four of us built the entire house.

Not long after we moved in, the back yard began to look like a little African plain. There was one large enclosure with trees, rocks and a pool and lots of little pens. Suzi and I would sit out on the back porch and watch the zoo animals graze. Many of these had been given to us by the overcrowded Knoxville Zoo, and some were mixed in with Pet Kingdom animals. It was nuts. What I couldn't sell of puppies, ducks, kittens, chickens, whatever—I'd bring home. Inside the house, we were constantly kept entertained by Jocamo the spider monkey, Joe the mynah bird and the parrots.

Suzi's attitude was always great, even if my shenanigans were sometimes a bit much. While she was breast-feeding

Kathaleen was at home with the animals from the time she was a baby. This is us in Hanna's Ark with a South American spotted leopard cat. (Jack Hanna)

Suzanne one day, I was across the family room bottle-feeding a baby chimpanzee who was very sick at the time. I didn't know if the chimp would come around with the formula, and I suddenly had a strange idea. Before I could open my mouth, Suzi had read my mind.

"No way, Jack," she said.

"What?" I said, kind of sheepishly.

"I know what you're thinking, and you can forget about it."

So much for that experiment. She told me later that she might have tried breast-feeding a sick primate if we'd been in the middle of Africa or something. But her main fear right then was that I'd tell the whole world. She was probably right.

Our favorite animals were the lion cubs we raised. The first one we ordered through Chase arrived at the airport in what we thought was too large a crate for an eight-week-old cub. It was winter, the case was covered up, and we couldn't really see inside. So we brought it home, into the kitchen. When we pried open the crate, we heard a roar inside, and this forty-pound animal jumped out and up onto the kitchen counter. This thing was at least five months old, and I wasn't about to play around on the floor with it. Carefully, we packed it back up and returned it.

Eventually, we had six baby lions behind the house. It was constant work hunting up meat to feed them. Mostly, I would find dying livestock, sick cows, at nearby farms. I didn't mind, because those cubs gave us a great learning experience and so much joy.

It was a great, hectic time in our lives. Once Hector, our wild goat, got loose in some rich lady's living room on the farm next door. We had to go with a friend and lasso him out. At Easter, I sold loads of baby chicks, telling the parents that they could bring them back to me when they grew too big. They all came back, and I wound up with chickens at home running around everywhere. If I couldn't sell a puppy within a few weeks, I'd bring him home. Suzi was having a ball—she didn't want to get rid of anything. Kathaleen played with the lion cubs in her crib, while Joe the mynah bird went around screaming "Aw, shit!"

Daisy was the first lion cub we owned and our most precious, beloved animal. She was a beautiful cat. Her temperament was that of a wild animal, but she also related to people. It wasn't long after we'd bought her from Chase that she became like a member of the family, staying with us at home, both inside and outside, riding in the car everywhere we went.

*D*aisy's cubs were everywhere, including *Kathaleen's crib.* (Jack Hanna)

When Daisy grew to her full size and weighed three hundred pounds, I had to keep her outdoors. Our relationship was similar to that of Elsa and Joy Adamson in *Born Free*, which, by the way, supplied the song that Suzi and I danced to on our wedding night. I'd go into her pen every day and talk to her real softly and she would vocalize—we were close. There just was no way I could ever imagine that one day, in one sudden moment, in less than half a second, she would all but destroy two families and break our hearts.

On that terrible day, Linda Ramsbottom brought her three-year-old son, Matthew, to the shop. Once Pet Kingdom became established, it was common for parents to bring their kids around, not necessarily to buy anything, but just to look at the animals. Mrs. Ramsbottom asked if it was possible to take Matthew to see my collection of animals back at the house, about eight miles away. I was busy at the store and didn't hesitate to tell her to go ahead. People were always coming out to see my animals. I thought it was safe, what with the protective outer fence around the animals.

The next thing I knew, about one o'clock in the afternoon, I received a phone call from my neighbor Mrs. Troglin. I can still hear her words, clear as a bell:

"Jack, you've got to come home right now—a little boy has lost his arm to your lion."

"What?" I thought I was hearing things.

"Daisy's taken a little boy's arm off," she said. "The police are on their way to pick you up."

This is Daisy shortly before the accident. Although she looks very gentle, you can tell from the size of her paw that she was a powerful animal.
(Tom Minter)

The police came by, not to arrest me, but because the arm was inside the enclosure and they couldn't get in there to get it out and take it to the hospital with the boy, where it might be reattached. The police cruiser arrived, I jumped in, and we screeched off down the road. We pulled up in the driveway about the same time as the ambulance.

The scene was unreal. The mother was, understandably, in a state of shock, but I'll never forget the little boy as long

After the accident, Daisy was moved to the Knoxville Zoo. I missed her, but I was happy when she had this litter of beautiful cubs right after she arrived at the zoo. (Jack Hanna)

as I live. He was standing there, not crying or anything, with a sheet wrapped around him—you could see the blood coming through and there was no arm. I just couldn't put this all together, the flashing lights, the sirens—it was like a bad dream.

Daisy was on the other side of the pen, looking no different than she ever did. I went into the pen and picked up the arm and brought it out and handed it to the medics. They rushed it to Children's Hospital—the boy had already gone ahead in another ambulance. Standing there, I felt totally lost for the first time in my life. What had I done to this three-year-old child? I guessed I had almost killed somebody.

The police took me to the hospital, and I waited and waited for news. It seemed like forever. Finally, around five o'clock, they came to tell me that they couldn't reattach the arm, that it wouldn't work, because Matthew could wind up getting gangrene, along with other complications. Dr. Bill Patterson, head of the Knoxville Zoo board, and Guy Smith, the Knoxville Zoo director, were both there. Guy was a great animal lover and also had raised a lion cub. The two of them helped me with the usual stuff—"it's not your fault," and all that. There was also Dr. Albert Chesney, a longtime family friend, who had experienced a similar tragedy, involving a child's death in an auto accident—he'd gone through hell, and his words helped greatly. At the time, nothing meant much to me, but looking back, their support helped me a lot.

My family was also very supportive, even though they were devastated. "What should we do with the lion?" my dad wanted to know. That night I went into the beautiful enclosure with Daisy and cried. I told her she was going to the zoo. I'd had her since she was six weeks old, but here it was two years and over three hundred pounds later, and a little boy had lost his arm. The next day, the zoo truck came to take her away.

I visited Matthew a couple of times in the hospital, but it

didn't work out. His family understandably didn't want me around, and the doctor and my attorney both thought it was best for me to stay away. Years later, in the early part of 1988, I was surprised by a wonderful letter from Mrs. Ramsbottom. She had just seen an article about me in *People* magazine, and she wanted to let me know that Matthew was a freshman at the University of Tennessee, that he loved swimming and girls, and that he was a typical teenager. That's the best letter I ever received.

But at the time, naturally, there were lawsuits, and they were long and messy. I had three different insurance policies, but none wanted to pay. Eventually, my attorney sued the insurance companies in order to settle for Matthew's family. Of course, no amount is worth the price of an arm and all of the suffering all of us underwent.

The exact details of what actually happened never came out, and I didn't care much at the time. But when I began to replay the episode, as I have so often over the years, I think I realized what probably happened. There were no bite marks, only teeth indentations on the arm. The boy had somehow gotten himself up against the chain fence and stuck his arm through it, maybe to pet Daisy. She probably just grabbed the arm, and with her power, jerked it right off.

With the story all over the local papers, life was very difficult for my entire family. Not long after the accident, Suzi and I were in a grocery line when we overheard some people talking—something to the tune of: "There's that Jack Hanna. He ought to go to prison for taking that boy's arm off."

Well, I looked at Suzi right then and there and said, "We're leaving." We had to leave Knoxville because we'd never be forgotten there. We just had to start over. The question was, where?

*T*wo spotted African leopard cubs and I pose in front of the Central Florida Zoo's new logo. (Jack Hanna)

3

STARTING OVER

Staying with the animal business was a tough choice. Besides the lion accident in Knoxville, I'd gotten hepatitis that same year from infected chimpanzees and lost twenty-five pounds in three weeks while staying in the hospital; also, I'd ruptured two discs moving animal crates at the pet shop, which resulted in back surgery. So it was easy for me to feel that maybe I'd taken a wrong turn careerwise.

But when Stan Brock told me about a job opening down South, working for Jim Fowler, one of the co-hosts of TV's *Wild Kingdom*, I couldn't resist. Fowler was in the process of assembling animals for Mattel's Circus World, a complex that was going up next to Disney World in Orlando. The animals were being held at a thousand-acre ranch in Albany, Georgia, and they needed somebody to help manage the place.

Before moving, I sadly returned the large part of my animal collection to the Knoxville Zoo. My remaining lions—Matthew, Mark, Luke and Sarah—I gave to a top-notch circus trainer from Europe, Wolfgang Holzmair, who was with the Ringling Brothers and Barnum & Bailey Circus. I had gone to see Holzmair's act and came away so impressed, I knew my cats would have a good home. People have a general misconception about circus animals being mistreated and underfed. This may have been true in the past and may still be so in some smaller troupes, but by and large circus animals are as well cared for as champion show dogs. Günter Gabel Williams of Ringling Brothers has the most beautiful cats in the world. You won't find any healthier tigers, or animals of any kind, for that matter.

Of course, all of our "household" pets, which were like immediate family, would move to Georgia with us. We packed up a pickup truck with two chimps, four macaw parrots, Jocamo the spider monkey, Willy the cat, Joe the mynah bird, our sheepdog and I forget who or what else. Suzi drove the station wagon with the children—one was sick, the other was breast-feeding. My mother was crying as we loaded up the truck, and I think at this point my dad was quite concerned about the direction my life was taking.

Without looking back, we headed out of Knoxville and down the road like the Walton family. I'd been to Georgia in advance and had arranged to have a house trailer ready for us, but when we got there after a tiresome trip, there was nothing on the site but a spigot in the ground. Fortunately, somebody put all of us up for the night, and the next day everything was miraculously taken care of by our only neighbors, Linda and Lew Thompson. A sewer was dug, the water put in, the trailer delivered and hooked up— everything. It seemed like such a long time since something had actually worked out right.

We lived in that trailer the whole time we were there, with a bedroom about the size of a desk for the kids and the animals bouncing around all over the place. It was like a dream—a good one. Outside, we had a thousand-acre ranch to ourselves. Hyenas, giraffes, zebras, baby elephants—the animals were all starting to come in. Suzi took care of the kids and picked pecans. I worked from daylight till dark with the animals. There weren't any cages, and we always had to watch for rattlesnakes—the place was loaded with them. I loved it anyway.

One of my first assignments when I got to the ranch was to go pick up three baby elephants at Kennedy International Airport. I was twenty-four years old, and had been to New York once before with Suzi for a couple of hours and hated it. My job was to fly up there, rent a truck, load up the elephants and bring them back.

With fourteen elephants on it, that jet was something else. They don't do this anymore—bring big jumbo jets from Africa with animals—but that day there were rhinos, elephants, and lions all getting off this plane at four o'clock in the morning. It was like an ark of the airways.

After the elephants cleared customs, we loaded them up and headed in the direction of New York City in order to go south. Not paying attention, I made a wrong turn and went somewhere where it said trucks weren't supposed to go. I was tired, I didn't see the sign—all I wanted to do was get headed toward Georgia, but obviously I screwed up.

Next thing I know, the top of the truck is stuck under an overpass. It was jammed in there pretty good. Fortunately there was stop-and-go traffic, so it just kind of wedged in. If I had been going fast, I would have torn the top right off. I got out to let some air out of the tires, the old trick. By this time, traffic was backed up a mile, and here came the police.

The cop was one of these no-nonsense guys. He jerked me out of the cab and told me to get in the back of the cruiser.

"You're goin' to jail," he barked at me. "Do you know that this costs the taxpayers a lot of money?" he screamed, pointing at the long line of honking cars. He kept yelling at me, telling me what an idiot I was. I couldn't even understand him, he was going a mile a minute.

"Can I tell you what's in the truck?" I asked him, real fast.

"Shut up!"

"If we don't get the back end open, those elephants are going to die." I slipped that in there real quick. What was he going to do? He wasn't going to kill me.

"What's going to die?" He looked at me like I was going to die.

"The elephants."

"Listen up, buddy. You get smart with me, you're gonna pay for it."

"They're going to die," I said real excitedly. "There's elephants in the back of that truck."

"That truck's too small for elephants."

"Baby elephants," I said. "That's what I've been trying to tell you."

"Now, you listen to me, son," the cop said, poking his finger in my chest. "We're going to open the back of that truck, and if there's no elephants in there, you're in real deep. You understand?"

Well, now he'd scared me, and I thought, damn, what if they're not back there anymore? So he pulled open the back door and these three blessed little trunks came squirming out of the dark. The cop's eyes got as big as grapefruits and he said, "I don't believe this. Those are the cutest things I ever saw."

Now his mind was off the traffic jam, the horns honking. All of a sudden, it was like I was talking to a different person. He asked me how old they were, what they ate.

"They're real babies," I said. Now I was talking and he was listening. "I've got to feed them a rice mixture every two hours, and that's why I'm worried, sir. My truck's stuck, but I don't care about the ticket—I've got to take these elephants down to Florida and get them their special feed."

He listened, real concerned, then said he thought he could help. He called for a special wrecker, and it came and lowered the tires and jerked the truck back out. The cop even had traffic stopped the other way so that I could turn the truck around. I thanked him; he never gave me a ticket. He even apologized—the whole ball of wax. And so, once again, I was on the road and, once again, the appeal of animals solved a tricky situation. It was a smooth ride with the elephants all the way back to Georgia, then on to Florida.

We spent six fantastic months on that ranch, and I learned a lot about animals—especially giraffes and elephants—from Jim Fowler. I had a great deal of one-on-one contact with the animals. Still, things didn't seem quite right. It was something to do with not having total control in making decisions about these animals, and a lot of other little things as well. I guess if I was going to be responsible, I wanted to run my own show. I wasn't about to quit, but I knew there wasn't a future there. When I was offered the directorship of a tiny zoo in central Florida, I had to go for it.

⋀⋀

Stan Brock turned me on to the zoo job in Sanford, Florida. It was 1973, and he had his own animal park in nearby Clermont. Down there, Stan and I became not just close friends but I guess what you might call "animal associates," in a business sense.

Stan was a former co-host on Marlin Perkins' *Wild King-dom*, and knew more about wild animals than anyone I'd ever met. He was a rugged guy, having spent seventeen years on a wilderness ranch in South America. I called on Stan often for advice in those days, and he was always there to help. I'm very thankful for that—I don't think you can do it in the animal business without some knowledgeable help along the way.

Again, I packed up the family and the animals and U-Hauled us all down the road. When we got to Sanford, I was a little bit let down. Having only seen the place once, I'd forgotten how small it was. Any zoo on an acre and a half is a crowded situation, but you tend to overlook that kind of thing when you want to direct your own zoo. The zoo's office was a cubbyhole on the sixth floor of a

Two-year-old Suzanne with tiger cub. (Suzi Hanna)

⋀⋁⋀⋁⋀⋁⋀⋁⋀⋁⋀⋁⋀⋁⋀⋁⋀⋁

bank building two blocks away. But I loved the fact that this place was so small, I thought of it as the neatest little zoo in America. I also started thinking about ways to expand.

The first thing I did was go in there and get the employees fired up, all four of them. I told them what a great place we had here and how we were going to expand and improve conditions. We had a fantastic animal selection, even if it was overcrowded. There were lions, tigers, jaguars, alligators, chimps, all kinds of birds and a little petting zoo. Oh yes, and rats. We really had a lot of rats. Most zoos have rats. They're naturally attracted to the feed, the concessions, and being on a river, as the zoo was, made it even worse.

In those two years at Sanford, we turned the place around pretty good, so good, in fact, that we wound up with a new zoo: the 104-acre Central Florida Zoological park on the shores of Lake Monroe. I moved on just after it opened, but I often think about all those lucky animals we moved. For

The old Central Florida Zoo, located on one acre in Sanford, Florida.
(Chamber of Commerce, Sanford, Florida)

*S*obik and Fat Boy the hippo shared a moat and became great friends. (Bob Frey)

them, it was like moving from the ghetto to a suburban estate.

Everything I accomplished in Florida was the result of plain old blind, youthful enthusiasm. One of the first things I did was go down the street to a man named John Sobik, who owned a string of successful sandwich shops, and ask him if he'd give me $5,000 to buy an elephant. I told him we'd name the elephant after him and tie him in to all kinds of promotions. He gave me the $5,000. So I drove down to Bill Chase and bought one of those baby Indian bull elephants that I always wanted. We brought Sobik back up in a pony trailer.

Stan Brock gave me a hippo, but I didn't know where to put it. So I took this nice little monkey island we had, moved the spider monkeys off and put Sobik and the hippo out there. They got along tremendously. I don't know if I'd ever do it that way again, but it sure worked well for us.

We had some funny incidents with that elephant. Of course, animal incidents—especially the ones where no one gets hurt—are always funnier in retrospect; at the time they just seemed crazy.

The "Pachyderm Pro-Animal" was one of my early promotional brainstorms. The idea was to have a charity golf tournament, a fund-raiser for the zoo. Instead of a "pro-am," this was a "pro-an." We had little elephant badges, elephants on the golf balls, etc. To kick it off, I was going to have the golfers greeted by an elephant and other animals on the first tee.

Just before the event was scheduled to start, Suzi and I loaded Sobik into his horse trailer, and someone else hooked it up to our brand-new station wagon. This was a mistake—always hook up your trailer yourself.

Following behind us was a character named Herbie Sullivan, the herpetologist. Herbie was my friend and co-worker and some piece of work. He had long sideburns and horn-rimmed glasses and drove a 1968 light blue T-bird convertible with light blue angel-hair interior. Herbie liked to be Mr. Big Time—he looked and acted the part. Herbie's main thing was snakes. He usually carried one with him wherever he went—his license plate read: SNAKE DR. (Herbie did know his snakes and went out of his way to tend to sick snakes.) On this day, Herbie had a pet raccoon with him, along with a boa constrictor in a box next to him on the seat.

So Herbie was behind us as we approached the golf course, which was about four miles from the zoo. Riding in the trailer with the elephant was Robbie Campbell, a zoo worker.

Suddenly, as we turned up onto the clubhouse road at about thirty m.p.h., the trailer snapped off, sideswiped the back of my new car and went flying across the golf course. The trailer crossed a fairway and crashed into a large white oak tree, popping the elephant right out the back. He took off running across the golf course, and I thought, oh no,

*F*at Boy the baby hippo, Sobik the baby elephant, who later went for a run on the local golf course, and myself. (Gary Taylor)

mass destruction on the links—headlines of scattered golfers and ruined greens.

Robbie staggered out of the trailer and said he thought
his ribs were broken. Herbie, cool as a cucumber, didn't
budge from his car and asked me why I let the elephant
trailer go out on the golf course. I was really upset.

"Do you think I arranged all this?" I yelled at Herbie. "We
got big problems. There's a hundred golfers waiting to tee
off, the elephant's loose on the course and Robbie's got
broken ribs. Do you think I did this on purpose?"

Herbie never got excited. He just sat there and said,
"Yep, I guess I'll go check Robbie out and then go up and
see how those models are doing." (He'd set it up to have
four local models tee the balls up on the first hole.)

"You're going to help me catch that damned elephant," I
told Herbie. "You're not going to play with your models or
your snake or anything else. If that elephant destroys this
course, the whole thing's going down the tubes."

Well, we called an ambulance for Robbie, and we chased
that elephant all over the course. We finally caught up to
him after he'd calmed down and was eating out of the rough
near the sixth green. It was two hours before any golfers
teed off, but I never saw any of it. I was too busy apologiz-
ing to the greenskeeper. The elephant was unhurt, but we
had some hoofprints to repair on one of the greens, which
cost us a couple hundred bucks. Of course, it could have
been worse.

I would do almost anything to raise money and awareness
for the zoo, and it was largely because of this and the
support of the local press that Sanford got its new zoo in
1975. One of the early fund-raisers was a birthday party for
Sobik that I threw at the old Orlando Sports Stadium. I got
a marching band, I got kids practicing gymnastics and I
called them a circus, which, of course, was a little exagger-
ated. Actually, they were training at a circus school in
Sarasota. This show was a real mix. I had karate demonstrations, I had attack-dog demonstrations and, of course, I

had a cake, which must have weighed over two hundred pounds.

The day before the party, Sobik got diarrhea real bad. Crap was flying everywhere. Now, an elephant with diarrhea is a serious thing—he can die. But I also had one of my biggest fund-raisers scheduled for the next day, with a couple thousand tickets sold (the place held about sixteen thousand). I called the vet over, and he told me that Sobik would be all right but if we wanted to have our party, we would have to shove these pills down his mouth. That's when I learned how smart elephants are.

Sobik wouldn't swallow the medicine. So we put it in an orange; he wouldn't eat the orange. So we laid out ten oranges. I had placed the pills in one of them—I had them hidden so deep that no adult human being could tell they were in there. That elephant ate every single orange but the one with the medicine. Did this twice in a row.

We finally got him to take his medicine by tricking him with some molasses on a big wooden spoon. By the time he realized the medicine was in there, the stuff was stuck to his tongue and had to go down.

Sobik's condition improved for his big day, but he still dumped on everything that moved. He even crapped on his own birthday cake. I have to admit, though, that it was worth a lot of laughs and helped make the event successful.

Sobik was a beautiful animal and a great source of entertainment, at least for most of us. Once I hired a character named Prince Rudolph Alexander, who said he was from Austria. Rudolph played the guitar and had a chimp show. He claimed he'd had his act on Johnny Carson. This wasn't true. He certainly was a con artist, but an entertaining one at that.

I'd built a platform on top of the elephant house for Rudolph to perform on while Suzi sold cotton candy. Even with his tattered uniform, his phony accent and his aging chimp, his show was all right—he'd have the chimp do four or five tricks, and people loved it.

One day, after he'd been with us about six months, I was introducing Rudolph as I always did, ". . . all the way from California and straight from the Johnny Carson show . . . ," when Sobik sneaked his trunk up to a ledge where Rudolph had laid down his guitar for a moment. The elephant snatched up Rudolph's instrument, put it on the ground and stomped it into splinters.

Rudolph got all red in the face and turned toward the crowd gathered for his act. "Ladies and gentlemen," he announced (he wore a little lavaliere microphone), "the elephant present has just destroyed my prized handmade Austrian guitar. I, as an artist, cannot continue to perform under these conditions. Therefore, I regret to inform you that I quit." We never saw him again.

⋀⋀

Because there was no local ASPCA (American Society for the Prevention of Cruelty to Animals) in Sanford, and

*R*udolph Alexander and Bongo the chimp.
(Chamber of Commerce, Sanford, Florida)

because the Fish and Game Commission was so busy, people would phone me whenever any kind of animal emergency came up. A typical example was the call I got from the police early one morning about a bear loose in Winter Park, an exclusive community outside Orlando. I didn't really want to believe this story, and I told the caller as much. That's when the chief got on the line and asked me would I please come over and help them get this bear.

All right, so I called good old reliable Stan, who brought along a set of heavy ropes and a tranquilizer gun. The

*R*udolph Alexander getting ready to perform on the top of Sobik's house.
(Beth Weilenman)

Winter Park cops sent us a motorcade and within minutes we were whizzing up to an address fifteen miles away. When we got there, there were already two fire trucks, a couple hundred spectators, Herbie, who was my assistant on everything (I had called him and asked him to bring the zoo truck, but naturally he'd brought his T-Bird), and a television news crew. The star of the show, a three-hundred-pound bear, was halfway up a tall white oak tree. Here was the biggest black bear I'd ever seen, right in the middle of this lady's yard in this exclusive neighborhood.

*B*ear capture in Winter Park. (Beth Weilenman)

"I say, Jack, that's quite some bear," said Stan in his usual, calm fashion. "We'll take care of this—should be no problem." He was actually smiling.

My first thought was, if that bear comes out of that tree and heads for the crowd, he could do some damage. The police had wanted to shoot the bear when they first got to the scene, but the neighbors had protested. That's when we got called in.

Stan fired his tranquilizer gun and hit the bear in the butt, but the dart had no effect. The bear just sat there. After two more direct hits, the bear shot out of that tree, full speed, and, to our relief, ran away from the people. He ran around for a half hour before he slowed down from the sedative. (Bears, by the way, are as fast as their reputation—when panicked or angry, they are lightning fast.)

We were chasing him, the police cruisers were chasing him—I remember at one point feeling like Marlin Perkins running through these lush yards. I felt like I was on a *Wild Kingdom* episode. I mean, here were the police letting us have the run of everything, telling everyone to stay away but us.

Stan was yelling stuff like "Jack, you go that way, I'll go this way." Fine, sounded like fun, but I thought, what if I go that way and run into the bear? I don't have the gun—

Stan does. All I have is the rope. I had these big glasses on and I must have looked like some dork.

When I thought I spotted the bear in another back yard, I yelled to Stan to stay nearby. Then, all of a sudden, in one big blur, I saw the bear burst into the open and go running right through the shallow end of this lady's pool. Just remembering the look on her face still cracks me up fifteen years later. She's sitting on her porch and sees a bear running across her yard, followed by me, with a rope, followed by Stan, with his gun—just your typical Chinese fire drill. It was like "What the . . . ?"

So we chased the bear down to a nearby lake area where Stan gave him another blast from the tranquilizer gun. He tried to swim away, but the fourth dart began to take effect (we realized later that the other darts hadn't worked because they landed in the bear's fatty tissue). We lassoed him from a motorboat, then dragged him up to land so he wouldn't drown.

By this time Herb was there with the zoo truck, and about four of us transferred the bear into one of these huge liquor storage cages I'd bought from the railroad. We took him to the zoo for temporary safekeeping. This whole adventure was big news the next day, and the day after that we had a record-breaking Monday at the zoo.

The bear was thought to be the offspring of a rare Himalayan sun bear that had escaped from a circus several years back. He'd probably come down from the Ocala National Forest forty or fifty miles to the north, probably just walked right along next to the freeway. We released him back into the forest three weeks later. It was all tremendous publicity for the zoo. I guess everybody loves a good animal story, and if I hadn't totally realized it before, that idea certainly clicked in then.

∧∧

Another thing about Florida was that we got a lot of problem calls about alligators. The expanding highway and building construction in the 1970s was often responsible for pushing alligators out of their natural habitats, sending them to all kinds of unlikely places—mostly swimming pools. They were sometimes a nuisance and sometimes dangerous. But as a zoo director in Florida, I soon found that "gators" was as much a part of my daily vocabulary as "cat" or "dog" might be to a vet.

One night the phone rang about 2 A.M. A twelve-foot-long alligator had its teeth stuck in the tire of a police cruiser in the Longwood Hotel parking lot. Apparently, the cops had tried to corral this wayward creature by using their cruiser to back him into a corner against a building. The poor thing had gotten mad and bitten into the tire, and now its jaws were locked on. They didn't know what to do. They couldn't shoot it, since alligators were endangered at the time. Besides, that wouldn't get the teeth loose.

I had to laugh; I also had to call Herbie, since he was our "herpetologist." Herbie had had too much rum and at first didn't want to get up. But once he got the scent of adventure, he was ready to go. He showed up with some ropes, and had thought out a plan to first lasso the gator, then pull him off the tire. Somehow I didn't feel like a cowboy.

We roped the alligator's head and pulled him loose, but at the same time, he flipped backward, knocking us both to the ground. Herbie got all entangled in his own ropes, but with the help of the cops, we managed to get the ropes off Herbie and onto the alligator. Once he was tied tight, we threw him in the back of my station wagon, which had just been repaired after the elephant fiasco. (Imagine, by the way, filling out claim forms and trying to convince an insurance adjuster that the damage was caused by an elephant escaping from a trailer on a golf course.)

The cops asked us where we were taking the alligator, and we told them the zoo, of course—which wasn't true. We were going to drop him off, as we always did, in nearby Lake Monroe. In my two years in Sanford, I must have sent more than a dozen rescued alligators back into that lake, since the zoo had no room for them. I liked to watch them waddle back into their watery home. Hey, boys, have a fun time, I'd say as they swam away.

∧∧

Zoo workers are generally dedicated and careful people, but sometimes animal thefts occur. At Sanford, someone was stealing exotic birds from the zoo. The three missing macaws were replaceable, though expensive, but it really upset me when they broke into my office and stole Joe, my prized mynah bird. These birds went for four to six hundred dollars at the time, but Joe was priceless. His routine ran from "What's the matter?" to "Hello" to "I wanna take your order" to "Aw, shit."

The police wanted to help me on this since Joe was such a kick and all the zoo visitors loved him. The local paper helped with a story that had the headline: "He's mine a bird, not yours."

Two weeks after the theft, I received a call from Michigan; it was a guy claiming to know where my bird was. He said that his cousin knew the person who stole Joe and that the bird was at a house on Pine Avenue near downtown Orlando. He wouldn't tell me who had the bird, he just gave me the address. Some lead.

I called the police and told them the story, and they said that without a search warrant they couldn't do anything. But they went ahead and staked out the house for a couple of days and got some results. They came to get me, said they couldn't get a warrant but that we were going to go knock on the door and ask the people nicely if they had my bird.

The lady at the door was nice enough; she said yes, they had bought a bird several days ago. The police told her they thought it might be mine. "Well, how do you know that?" she asked us.

I said, "Ma'am, I'll tell you what I'll do. I don't even want to see the bird. You put the bird in this room right here, and I'll go in the other room, and I will talk to that bird. He's going to say 'Aw, shit' and 'I wanna take your order.' "

A fourteen-foot anaconda tries to swallow my finger ... (People Weekly, Bob Frey)

So they put the bird on the other side of the door, and I said, "Hey, Joe, what's the matter?" He heard my voice and didn't hesitate. "Aw, shit," he said. When I asked him "What's the matter?" again, he came back with "I wanna take your order."

Right then, the policeman said, "That's it. It's your bird."

I went home with Joe. The lady was nice about it. She could have refused, and we would have had to go to court over the bird and I might never have gotten him back, though we probably would have had a few laughs in court.

Joe went everywhere with me, especially on my fund-

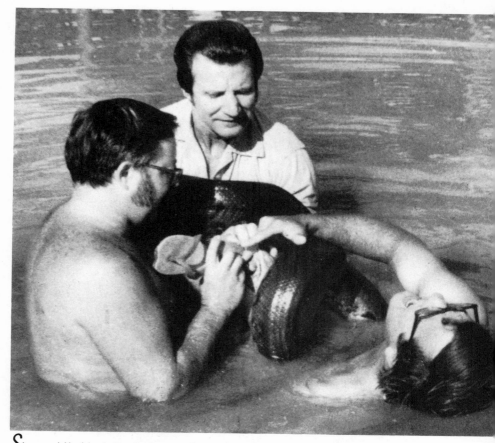

*S*tan and Herbie, trying to free my finger... *(People Weekly,* Bob Frey)

raising speeches. Once, I was about to speak at a church in front of three hundred potential zoo donors. "Before we hear from Mr. Hanna," said the minister after introducing me, "please join me in a little prayer."

"Aw, shit," Joe screeched, loud as ever.

During my last few months in Florida, I got involved in a movie deal with Stan and a group of other people. The film was called *The Forgotten Wilderness*, and I guess you could say it was like the title, all but forgotten. Eventually, I would lose the money I invested in it, but that's not so bad. What

*S*obik knocking a hole in the wall of his house at the old Central Florida Zoo. (Beth Weilenman)

*F*at Boy the hippo being transported to the new Central Florida Zoo. (Beth Weilenman)

really would have made me mad would have been losing a finger to the big snake that was one of the stars of the movie. It was a close call.

The snake, a fourteen-foot, 120-pound anaconda, was used in an animal-capture scene that was being shot in a local pond. Most of the filming was done in South America, but some of the close-ups of the animal scenes were shot in Florida. I was helping out on location, and I noticed that the snake had a loose piece of skin dangling from his nose. I went to pick it off, maybe a little too casually, and the snake just sucked up my finger, clamped right down on it.

"Don't move your finger, or you'll lose it," said Stan. I couldn't really move it anyway—it was like having it stuck in a vise with sharp teeth, about 220 of them. While I screamed in pain, Stan and Herbie—who was there for snake advice—tried to pry my finger loose.

Meanwhile a guy from the local newspaper was going nuts taking pictures, instead of helping out. Stan got him to put down his camera and go get something to jam in the snake's mouth so I could get the finger out. He did, and I was able to pull my finger back while Stan and Herbie held the snake's jaws open wide.

Miraculously, the finger was all there. Oh, it was shredded pretty good and had about two dozen punctures, some all the way through, but it was still attached. They took me to the hospital and insisted on giving me shots against infection, even though the snake wasn't poisonous. The shots in my butt wound up hurting worse than my finger.

∧∧

In 1975, I left central Florida without a lot of fanfare but with a very positive feeling. The new zoo had just opened, thanks to many people, on the Fourth of July, and I had a large emotional investment in that. After my two great years at Sanford, I was leaving to go into the animal-film business, a venture that I thought at the time was going to set me off on a lucrative new career. I was wrong, but that's all right. Indirectly, it got me one step closer to Columbus.

Julie with Flopsy, her favorite bunny, at age six when she was just getting off chemotherapy. (Columbus Zoo file)

4

BACK
TO
THE
WILD

They say you can't go home again, which is
something I finally found out on my second move back to
Knoxville. While Suzi and our three daughters waited back
in Florida, I also found out I wasn't going to be the next
Walt Disney. Six months of going out on the road promoting *The Forgotten Wilderness* turned out to be an effort best
forgotten. With the movie business behind me, I returned
home to Knoxville, with the hopes of coming up with
something to make ends meet.

My father suggested that I go into the real estate business, and with a family and no money, who was I to argue?
My dad reasoned that since I was outgoing and a good
salesman, I'd be a cinch to be a successful realtor. The only
problem was the difference between selling something you
want to sell—in my case, anything to do with animals—
and something you're indifferent to.

I was very fortunate at the time to hook up with Harold
"Bubba" Beal, a Knoxville realtor who was interested in my
dad's property, the beautiful farm I grew up on. For tax
purposes, Dad wanted to sell, and as one-third owner, I
entered into a limited partnership with Bubba. We decided
to turn the old homestead into a restaurant (Hanna's), and
we used the rest of the property to build seventeen homes.

At first, I was very happy and relieved, but it didn't take me long to lament the fact that I was totally removed from something I'd loved all my life: animals. Before long, I would remedy this.

Meanwhile, I purchased a modest brick house near my brother's farm and sent for Suzi and the kids. It was Friday, on Memorial Day weekend, when the moving van arrived from Florida. We had the movers put everything in the garage and decided to wait until the next day to bring it in—a Saturday I'll remember as long as I live.

Suzi and I got up early and began moving furniture and boxes around, making a fair amount of noise. After a while, we noticed that Julie, who was then two years old, was sleeping way too late on the couch. Suzi felt her forehead, and it was practically on fire—she had a 105-degree temperature.

We rushed her to Children's Hospital in Knoxville, but our family doctor couldn't diagnose the problem at first, and he couldn't control the fever either. On Sunday, her condition worsened, and the doctors decided to do a bone-marrow test. The results were devastating. They told us that little Julie had leukemia. By this time, she had already developed pneumonia and a staph infection due to her lack of immunity.

Our doctor told us that, since Julie was going downhill so fast, the best thing to do was get her to St. Jude's Hospital in Memphis, some 450 miles away, as fast as humanly possible. But that was so far and we had so little time. I called Bubba, since I knew he was a pilot, and in a few hours he flew us in a twin-engine plane to Memphis. If we had driven her, she might have died, since time was so precious.

Upon her arrival, Julie was placed in a sterile intensive-care unit, where she spent the next two months in isolation to protect her from infectious diseases. It was a long, slow ordeal for everyone, but gradually, the chemotherapy treatments, radiation, bone-marrow treatments and spinal taps were successful, and Julie beat the odds. Her leukemia has been in remission ever since, and for that, our entire family is very thankful.

The Knoxville Zoo had always supported me, even at the time of the lion incident that caused me to leave town three years earlier. Now that I was back in town, they asked me to be on the board of trustees of the Appalachian Zoological Society, a support arm of the zoo. Of course, I accepted, since this was just the shot in the arm that I needed to get reinvolved with the animal world.

About that same time, Stan Brock called me with an idea that would also get me back into the kind of work I loved. His timing was perfect, and his idea was intriguing and exciting. Stan's plan was to take two adult jaguars from American zoos where they were born and transport them to the South American jungle where their parents were born. There, after a period of acclimatization, they would be released into the wild.

Together, Stan and I founded the Freedom for Animals Fund, a nonprofit organization dedicated to the reestablishment of threatened and endangered species in their natural habitats in the wild. This is an idealistic common goal of modern-day zoos, but one that's all too seldom realized. It's basically the opposite of what the old zoos set out to do—instead of grabbing 'em out of the wild, let's take 'em back.

This project would take over a year to realize, and before we were done, it would involve an entire community, two zoos, Alcoa, the U.S. Fish and Wildlife Service, the Venezuelan and Haitian governments and, most importantly, Bubba Beal, since he was the one who flew us down there, in his own plane.

The longest wait was for the permits. During this time, I continued to work with Bubba, and like so many people who have been around me over the years, he was bitten by the animal bug. One day, after he overheard me talking to Stan about the project, Bubba offered us the use of one of his planes, an old 1937 Grumman Goose amphibian. This was the perfect flying machine for our needs—now all we had to do was find gas money.

On the other end, Stan had put it together with Dr. Pedro Trebbau, a Venezuelan wildlife authority. Dr. Trebbau knew a conservationist rancher in the remote Apure Llanos region who would build a $10,000 chain link fence around a four-acre compound for the cats, where they'd be held temporarily before being released into a 190,000-acre animal sanctuary.

Guy Smith, the director of the Knoxville Zoo, offered Esther, a female jaguar, and we obtained the other one, Mato Grasso, a male, from the Central Florida Zoo. Both zoos were solidly behind our plan—and not every zoo would so easily give up a jaguar, which is an endangered species. Alcoa, located just outside Knoxville, gave us two beautiful steel crates that they had custom-built for transporting the animals. As for the gas money, that came from the Appalachian Zoological Society.

On November 14, 1977, we finally took off from Knoxville's Downtown Island Airport with one jaguar in tow and another to pick up. We ran into some minor engine trouble on the first leg of our trip to Florida, and when we finally left the States with our second jaguar, we were over a day late, creating a serious problem for our clearance papers to refuel in Haiti. That, and the fact that our cargo alarmed the Haitian authorities, created more delays, and we were more than two days late when we thankfully arrived in Caracas.

Stan Brock, of TV's Wild Kingdom, *with one of the jaguars we released into the wild in the Amazon River Basin in South America.*
(Doug Morris)

Dr. Trebbau met us there in his own plane, and our next step was to just "follow him" for a two-and-a-half-hour flight over jungle interior. It was thick and mountainous, seemingly never-ending, until we suddenly came to a small clearing in the jungle, a little grass strip with Indians running all around.

We landed the two planes and took the jaguars by tractor and trailer to their new enclosure a few miles away. I was very relieved that the animals were in perfect shape, not a scratch or skin burn anywhere. We went to check out the pen and it was ideal—situated around a swamp on some high ground.

At first, we couldn't get one of the cats to come out of its crate and into the compound. No one seemed alarmed, but I was concerned about getting out of there before nightfall. I was wearing L. L. Bean pants and, like Stan, I had on a safari shirt. I was trying to be Mr. Cool, but I was sweating like a monkey, and the insects were chewing me up. I couldn't have lived one day out there. I thought he was crazy, but Stan somehow reached into the crate and brought that full-grown jaguar out. I couldn't believe it—with one arm, he actually grabbed its tail and gently pulled it out.

The reintroduction, to be supervised by Dr. Trebbau, provided for the animals to be fed in the enclosure every night, just like in captivity. After a month, they'd still get their meals, but the gate would be left open. The idea was for them to stray a little farther each day, then come back at night. The next month, they'd be fed only every other day, then after that, twice a week. One day they wouldn't come back.

Eventually, the cats would begin by eating some easy prey, like armadillos and turtles, then move on to the bigger stuff, like deer and tapirs. The jaguars were strong and adaptable and should make it. We hoped that ultimately they would propagate.

We lifted off with a great feeling of accomplishment, yet without knowing if the project would end successfully. On the surface level, it didn't. One animal was found a year

Jaguar comes out of his crate into the pen where he would live for one month while being reintroduced into the wild. (Doug Morris)

later, killed and skinned by poachers, and the other one disappeared, even though it was equipped with a radio collar.

But in another sense the project was very successful. The concept was really nothing new and the work required by the project was formidable; obviously, we can't go releasing all sorts of zoo animals back into their natural habitats—there are too many physical and financial limitations. But animals in captivity are ambassadors to their cousins in the wild, and with every effort zoos make to represent the wild world of animals, the better people can appreciate wildlife and do their best to conserve it.

Bubba had some hairy moments after he agreed to carry a half dozen sick Indians on the flight back to Caracas (I was fortunate to be on Dr. Trebbau's plane). The plane was overloaded and barely got off the ground. As it gained altitude, it mowed the top of the tree line. When Bubba brought the landing gear down in Caracas, bushes and branches came pouring out onto the runway. Drugs were just getting big at the time, and the Goose was immediately surrounded by police, who were hardly impressed with any story about returning jaguars to the wild. After a couple hours of fast talking—and some checking up by the authorities—they finally cleared everybody.

The return to the States was uneventful, except for Bubba's little side trip to practice water landings on some lakes down in Florida. He scared the daylights out of us, but it was fun.

∧∧

Planning and carrying out the trip to South America was a big break for me. I had missed the excitement, the interaction with the animals—I missed speaking to people about animals. I love to talk about animals. But on my return, I went right back into the real estate thing and it just didn't work out. Suffice to say that I wasn't any Donald Trump.

Bubba was great all the way. During that time, he even got me involved in putting together a petting zoo on three acres behind a shopping center he'd invested in near Gatlinburg. It was a beautiful little area built around a mountain stream. I had a bear, some beavers, some mountain goats, and many exotic birds on display, and I always looked forward to my drive over there every other day.

Bubba gave me the opportunity to sell real estate and still read my animal books during working hours. He knew that

BABY ANIMAL KINGDOM

SEE
**Baby Lions, Camels, Llama, Zebra,
Bear, Monkeys, Giraffe and Many More**
Plus the
Farm Yard Petting Area
SEASON: June 9 - Oct. 23
HOURS: 9:30 A.M. - 7:30 P.M.

Pigeon Forge, Tennessee
(LOCATED ACROSS FROM MOUNTAIN OCEAN ON HWY. 441)

The "Baby Animal Kingdom" brochure. (Jack Hanna)

I loved animals and that I was in a very difficult period in my life, with no income and no zoo. And even though Julie was in remission, there was still the haunting knowledge that there was no such thing as a cure for leukemia. Things were very frustrating at the time, but he understood.

One day I was sitting in my office reading *International Wildlife* when Bubba walked in and said, "Jack, you're not happy doing this. You wouldn't be happy doing this even if you were making a million dollars." I had even tried to hide the magazine.

"You love your animals," he said. "Why don't you try and find something? You can stay here as long as you want."

It was a stroke of fate when Stan Smulewitz, an old friend, called me from New Jersey the very next day. Stan and I had once made fish tanks together; he left when the fish tanks started blowing apart and I got sued, but that's another story. Stan called to tell me that his sister, who lived in Columbus, Ohio, had seen an ad in the paper there for a zoo director. Maybe I was interested? Was I interested? Does a monkey eat peanuts. Does a hippo like water? Does a bear sleep in the woods?

My first family picture at the Columbus Zoo, November 1978.
(Columbus Zoo, Susan Scherer)

5

HELLO, COLUMBUS

The jump to being director of the Columbus Zoo was the biggest thing that had ever happened to me in my life—like going from dogcatcher to mayor without running for office. I had never been in charge of more than a dozen employees, and now I was overseeing ninety. When I got to Columbus, the annual budget was around $2 million—it's up to $7 million today—compared to the $250,000 budget I had to work with back in Florida. I was really diving into this thing, and I remember thinking at the time, either I'll make it go or I'll sink like a weighted toad. I had nothing to lose, and I never was one for just treading water.

All right, so my first impressions of the Columbus Zoo were made up of problems or, really, of challenges that presented themselves. Sitting behind my desk in the back of an old bird house on that very first day, I thought, let's map this out. What's the perception here? How is this zoo perceived by the community, by the trustees, by the employees, by the zoo world? To all of these I asked myself, what's the perception?

It's really just simple business. For example, you're taking over a gas station that's not making much money—obviously, you're not getting the right customers. A zoo is no different. I applied some common sense and a few simple business techniques—forget zoological techniques for now; somebody had already tried that and it didn't work. Just get back to fundamentals and try to get this zoo up and going.

You have to take care of that gas station, that zoo—first off, get it painted and fixed up, get your employees in nice uniforms. Have them go out there and say, "Hi, how you doin'? Can I fill it up? Can I tell you about the elephants? the giraffes?" Instill a sense of pride!

Whether it's your public or your staff, people will always be skeptical at first, but you have to fight this, you have to build some enthusiasm. You've got to get people to believe. And they will. Enthusiasm is infectious, just look at any winning team, whether it's Apple Macintosh or the L.A. Lakers.

An important change was happening in Columbus Zoo politics at the time, and that was the transfer of the Columbus Zoo from the Sewers and Drains Department to the Parks and Recreation Department. All Sewers and Drains cared about was that the animals weren't starving to death and that the ASPCA wasn't going to close the place down—that was the extent of their concern.

Mel Dodge, then head of Parks and Recreation, initiated the change. He was one of the main people responsible for hiring me, and has served as my godfather throughout my years in Columbus. Back in my first year, I went to Mel for advice on just about everything. If I didn't, it was because I knew he'd approve. Of course, I've made some mistakes along the way, but Mel always supported me. As far as people and animals are concerned, we usually see eye to eye.

Mel loves animals and loves people who love animals. He's had a number of his own lions over the years, and unofficially, he's been known to take an animal home overnight from the zoo now and then. But most importantly, Mel knew everything that went on at the zoo; he knew all the keepers by name, he knew what their jobs were, what all their special projects were. He would stop to chat with them about any animal—about care, feeding and breeding. There were major problems with morale at the zoo, and Mel knew it. But he gave me the confidence to go about things my own way, which is probably the same way he'd have done it if he'd been zoo director.

The easiest way to run any organization is to shut the door and do it all by yourself. You can leave all the problems outside and let them boil up to the point where the whole thing explodes. With this philosophy, either you or your organization will soon be gone . . . if you're lucky, you'll go first. I honestly don't know how they'd kept the lid on the Columbus Zoo. A zoo with malcontented employees taking care of wild animals is a powder keg.

Mel Dodge and I going over the ten-year master plan for the new Columbus Zoo in 1978. (Columbus Dispatch)

What I had to do immediately was to win the respect of the employees. I knew it wouldn't be easy; three-quarters of them were older than I was and had been there many years. And here I was, a nobody kid coming from a small zoo in Florida. Their main problem, as I saw it, was one of self-esteem. They thought no one cared about them or their animals. They felt the public and some trustees considered them "shit shovelers," which wasn't true.

The closed-door policy that existed had to go. In my first meeting with the zoo staff, I gave them a pep talk about how great this place could become—something none of them really believed. Their eyes were like lasers boring through me. I realized why the trustees hadn't bothered to introduce many of the staff on my previous visits before being hired. It was like a secret society, with everyone all clammed up.

I told them that I wanted them all—regardless of their function, be it keeper or garbage picker-upper—to give me a list of their problems, to tell me how they felt the zoo could be improved. Only about twenty or so lists came back, but I went to work on each one right away. I didn't want anyone to think his or her problem wasn't worthy of attention.

Money was always needed for this and that—for painting, for wood for the sides of buildings—money we didn't have. I tried to get people to donate paint, materials, anything. I gave Ken Cooke, the treasurer, fits. He's a zoo trustee, and like all trustees, a volunteer, only he had to work harder than most just trying to keep tabs on me. He would try to raise the budget, try to help in every way, but I didn't help him much. He was always saying, "Jack, you can't do this—the zoo hasn't got the money."

One thing I noticed about the zoo staff was that they all cared very much about their animals. I figured if I could come in with something big for the animals, the staff would pick up on it, the public would benefit and it would have a snowballing positive effect for everyone. The question was, what kind of splash could I make with little or no money?

If I didn't know then that anything is possible, I would soon find it out with a scheme that to this day makes me as proud as anything I've ever done.

The gorillas had always been the star attraction at the Columbus Zoo. Even with a run-down operation, our collection of great apes was generally held in high esteem throughout the zoo world. It seemed a shame to me that they were largely ignored by the community—like having Pavarotti sing with our local opera to an empty house. It was zoologically important, but few people cared that Colo, the zoo's oldest female, who was then twenty-one, was the first gorilla born in captivity.

When I got to Columbus, neither Colo nor any of the other apes had ever been outdoors on grass or felt the sunlight in a natural habitat. This wasn't anything unusual in zoos at the time, but I wanted to do something about it. I also knew that attendance jumps radically when you put animals in natural habitats.

When I came across an item in the paper about a man named John McConnell, the self-made multimillionaire founder of Worthington Industries, I thought, why not? He seemed like a community-type guy. Maybe this man would donate the money for us to build a new gorilla enclosure.

Getting directly in touch with Mr. McConnell was nearly impossible, since he had people from all sides asking for one thing or another. Fortunately, I was able to get to Joe Stegmayer, who is now his vice president and right-hand man. After several of my phone calls, he told me to come on over.

Joe was a man for detail, and I think at first I may have put him off with my vagueness. "Joe, I've got this idea," I told him right off the bat. "Our gorillas have never known anything but a concrete cage and bars; they don't know what grass is. I want to put the gorillas outside. It's going to be spring soon, and I've got to do something quick." I realized later I was talking to a man who had never even been to the zoo. Later, he was to become chairman of our zoo board.

I told him about an old, out-of-use elephant yard, now housing kangaroos, that could be turned into a gorilla environment. I told him that I had a plan drawn up, that we were going to raise the wall four feet on the outside, knock down the inside walls and install glass for viewing inside. I told him the whole thing would cost $40,000 or $50,000.

"What makes you think these gorillas aren't going to jump out?" he asked me.

"I just don't think they will," I said.

"You want us to give money in our name to put these gorillas outside. You realize if something happens, if they get out—it's our money that did it."

John McConnell gives the first major donation to Bongo to build a new gorilla exhibit, which helped turn the zoo around. (Columbus Dispatch)

"No, Joe, they won't," I told him, but he didn't seem very encouraged or enthusiastic. He said he'd call me.

Over the next three weeks, I called him all the time. I was so excited, and I think my enthusiasm got to him. Finally, Joe called *me* up and asked me to come in and meet Mr. McConnell.

John McConnell had a friendly look about him, not at all what I'd imagined. He was like a Santa Claus without a beard, a nice bubbly face. When I walked into his office, he was smoking a pipe. He just sat there and looked at me for about ten seconds without saying anything. I was very nervous.

"I've been hearing some stuff about the zoo," he said at last. "Joe tells me you're trying to do some good things over there." He put me on the positive side right away.

I told him, "Yes, sir," and reiterated my grandiose plan about building an outside yard for the gorillas. At the same time, I went into my usual speech about how the zoo is there for the use of everybody in the community: children, senior citizens, the handicapped or disabled. I always try to tell everybody that.

He listened, then told me he liked my plan, but he, too, was concerned about the gorillas escaping. "What makes you think they won't get out?" he asked. "I want somebody to check it out."

"I'm going to check it out, sir," I told him. "I've got a heck of an idea. Chimpanzees are the most ingenious and agile of all the zoo animals. I'm going to turn a chimp loose in there, and if he can't get out, I know a gorilla won't. It's got to work."

What I didn't tell Mr. McConnell later was that the chimp actually did get out. He ruined our test by going up and over the side of a portable wall. By that time, I had already announced the opening day of the new exhibit, so I didn't want to blow everything. We just put some hot wire over that corner and everything was all right.

Building the gorilla yard took 120 days, and I think that

during that time I began to win the respect of my employees, or most of them at least. We were indebted to Mr. McConnell, of course, but the entire exhibit was staff-designed and staff-built. That's what made everyone so proud—we did it ourselves.

To the newspapers and television, I built up a steady stream of PR for our project. May 19, 1979, was our big day, and as people heard about it, they became involved. We were all pushing together to get this thing ready in time. During this period, we were all becoming a team, working night and day and getting to know each other.

Gorilla people, who never cared too much about what went on in the rest of the zoo, now worked with maintenance people; aquarium people came in—nobody had ever known they existed. I was in there painting, shoveling sand, doing whatever I could. They all found out that everybody's success depends on everybody else's hard work at the zoo.

We finished just in time on May 18, and the next day was the biggest day of my life. The gorillas were afraid at first. They didn't want to come out. They'd peek out, then maybe take their hand or foot and touch the grass, pick up little pieces and put it in their mouths. It was sad, in a way. The first day only two of them came out into the new yard. Airplanes above bothered them a lot. They had never seen anything fly, and they were frightened. When a bird flew close by for the first time, they ducked. There's so much for animals in captivity to adapt to, even just being put out in a new yard.

But the whole project was a tremendous beginning for me—from the day John McConnell gave us his commitment to the day the first gorilla saw sunshine. It was also a great start for the community to become involved with the Columbus Zoo. But I was anxious those first days. I couldn't sleep at night thinking a gorilla might jump over that frigging wall.

We've spent millions of dollars in construction since then, but not a week goes by that I don't refer back to our staff's having built the gorilla exhibit for $50,000. As for the donation from Mr. McConnell, it began to set a new standard and it also paved the way for zoo charities and donations over the past ten years. I rode on it at the time, and I'm still riding it today.

*S*eldom Seen the snow monkey with some of his family.
(Columbus Zoo, Nancy Staley)

6

MONKEYS
ON
THE
INTERSTATE

While the gorillas seemed to be enjoying the outdoor life, and while community enthusiasm continued to grow, I knew I had to keep coming up with new ideas, new ways to upgrade the zoo. Just after the gorilla exhibit opened to such success, I thought, why not do the same thing with the snow monkeys?

Our ten snow monkeys, or Japanese macaques, were one of our finest attractions, but they were confined to indoor living—actually they were all romping around a big old cage. I thought, why not put the snow monkeys—who are very active and put on quite a show—out on this moated area called Monkey Island? At the time, this exhibit, which was the oldest at the zoo, was being used for small primates and goats. Now, I'm not saying those monkeys should have been left inside, but this is one scheme I wish I had never tried.

The plan was to fix up this old outdoor exhibit, get the monkeys outside, let the people see them better and make everybody happy. Before moving the monkeys, I had the moat filled with water and the wall raised outside the moat. I knew these monkeys could swim, I just didn't know how well. I guess I should have read up a little more—that's one of my failings.

Here I am in the moat. Seldom Seen Senior and Junior swam the moat and climbed over the wall on the hose. (Columbus Zoo, Earl W. Smith III)

Japanese snow monkeys not only swim, they swim on top of the water, underwater, they could swim in ice water—they love to swim. They can also climb hoses that are left out (to fill the moat), and, as we realized too late, that's exactly what a couple of our monkeys did. During a seven-month odyssey across central Ohio, they became the most notorious escapees the zoo has ever had.

I first heard about the "breakout" over my trusty little walkie-talkie that we all carry around the zoo. Escaped animals usually stick around near where they get out, since the zoo's their home. Our two monkeys (actually three escaped but one came back) were first spotted high up in some large trees on the edge of the river, just off the zoo grounds. They were about fifty feet up in some big old willow trees, virtually unreachable.

Since we had no veterinarian on the grounds at the time, no tranquilizer guns that worked well and no Tarzan on hand, I thought, let's get a chain saw, cut these trees down and see if we can get this over with quick. Bad idea.

The tree could fall either way, so I had one guy next to it with a net, while a zookeeper and I were out on the river in a rickety old rowboat with another net. The tree fell into the water with a huge splash, just missing the boat. By instinct, my keeper jumped into the water to grab the monkeys. This was a bad move; this guy was so eager to capture the monkeys, he forgot he couldn't swim!

I jumped into the river to try and save him, but when I hit the water, an underwater branch from the tree caught me in the groin area. Now I was moaning, my keeper was gasping for air and the monkeys were casually swimming upstream. By the time we got ourselves back together, they were long gone.

Over the next few weeks, the monkeys were spotted on farms a few miles from the zoo in an area near Seldom Seen Road, so I named them Seldom Seen Junior and Senior. They were foraging in people's gardens and having the time of their lives. By now, a lot of jokes were being made, the newspapers were covering it day by day and, of course, the local television newscasters were having a ball with it, too. I wasn't laughing, and I wasn't sleeping much either.

Some calls I received were from irate people, some even threatening to shoot the monkeys if they didn't stay out of their gardens. I begged them not to, to please have patience; I promised that we would capture the monkeys.

Most of the calls I got were from people enjoying this "great escape." You had to figure that a lot of these people were rooting for the snow monkeys to stay out there as long as possible. A woman told us she'd been watching one monkey sit in her crab apple tree eating fruit; another said he was swimming in her pond. One man told us the animal had been sleeping in his toolshed at night. With every sighting, we'd go up there and come back empty-handed; some of them may have been false alarms. Half the time, we never even knew which monkey we were chasing, not that it mattered.

For about a month, we lost track of the monkeys. We

figured they had left the area, since the calls stopped coming. The story sort of died down, but I knew those monkeys were still out there. They were quite hardy, and I knew they could survive in the "wild" of Ohio in the summer. They were also developing muscles they'd never used before and could be quite dangerous, especially if cornered by people who didn't know what they were doing.

Then, one night, some five weeks after they got out, Senior somehow worked his way back to the zoo, to the original bunch of trees next to his enclosure. We called Dr. Gardner, our veterinarian, to the scene with tranquilizer guns. He managed to hit him twice, with no effect. With the help of twenty-two people and five floodlights, we cut down two more trees in an attempt to nab him before we wound up watching him swim to the other shore and head north.

Cutting down all these trees just added to my embarrassment, and I heard from Mel Dodge about that. Now we were decimating our local woods. I mean, what was this, the Keystone Kops? Can't anybody catch those monkeys?

From time to time, truck drivers would help us keep track of Seldom Seen Senior and Junior. We had a map in my office with pins on it, as if we were charting enemy troop movements during a war. We put pins in every day. Gradually, it became apparent that Senior and Junior were separately moving north along I-71, each on different sides of the interstate, about twenty miles apart.

One day a trucker called to tell us he'd tried to get Senior inside the cab of his truck by offering him a sandwich. Senior ate the sandwich, then bolted to a nearby golf course. He seemed content out there, so I sent some keepers to the course with a new plan.

I knew that the minute Senior spotted the zoo uniforms he would hightail it out of there, so I had the keepers dress up like golfers and put tranquilizer guns in their golf bags, along with golf clubs, of course. I even told them to be sure they were playing golf, since Senior was so smart. I was getting desperate.

When the keepers spotted him in a tree, they stayed calm, finished their shots like I told them, then went to their bags for the guns. The moment Senior saw them with the guns, he was off like a bullet. Bye-bye.

An earlier plan I'd had, when the monkeys were still near Columbus, was to lure them back with a female, which I would let loose in the general area. I called Mel Dodge to ask him what he thought. No good, he said—you'd probably end up with three monkeys at large. What if they managed to breed the female without getting caught and you ended up with an entire colony of Seldom Seens up there? Good point. All right, so we dropped that one.

Eventually, by late fall, the monkeys made it all the way up to Upper Sandusky and Cleveland. They'd traveled over a hundred miles from the zoo. It appeared that now that the vegetable gardens were empty, with winter coming on,

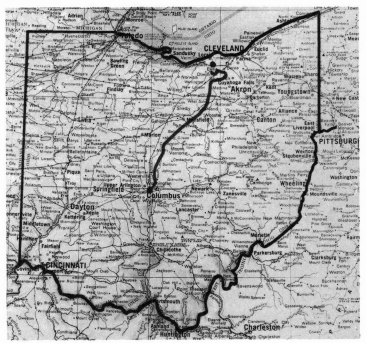

*M*ap. (Jack Hanna)

they were ready to return to civilization, on their own terms anyway. The sightings were becoming more frequent and always around people.

In Upper Sandusky, a father and son were out hunting for raccoons when either Junior or Senior jumped out of the woods and really scared their dog. One guy had one of the monkeys trapped in his kitchen before it burst loose through a window. I was cursing these animals day by day. I was also starting to worry that now that they were in the suburbs a child was going to be bitten.

In the second week of November, almost six months after they escaped, we got Junior back thanks to a tip from a county game warden near Upper Sandusky. With a number of zoo staff, we surrounded the barn where he was hiding and took him in relatively easy fashion. I felt a little better, but Senior was still at large, and I knew he wasn't going to come in easily. I remember telling the press, however, that it was just a matter of time until we'd get him (the question was, how long?). "We always get our monkey," I told them after Junior was captured. Think positive.

I was by this time getting a little edgy with my staff. I was tired of people coming back empty-handed, of overtime pay, of nighttime hours, of the Columbus Zoo—and its new director—being the laughingstock of the entire community.

Tommy Steele, one of our keepers, was one of the "bounty hunters" I'd sent out from time to time. Tommy lived just across the river, was in his early twenties and had worked around the zoo since he was a little boy. I'll never forget the night of the call from Elyria, a Cleveland suburb. The sheriff's department had called to tell us that Senior was trapped in a garage and that they would wait for us to come to get him. I wanted to go really bad, but I couldn't leave the zoo because of an important giraffe birth. I had a talk with Tommy before he left.

"Mr. Hanna," Tommy told me, "I'll come back with him this time. I'll get him."

"Please, Tommy. Get him for me, will you?" I was half pleading, half ordering. We couldn't take another blunder. I think I may have said "dead or alive," half jokingly, but I knew Tommy wouldn't shoot the monkey.

"That monkey ain't gettin' away from me, for better or worse. I'll get him. I promise." He had a net, a crate, everything. He looked determined. I told him to call me when he got up there.

When Tommy got to the house (owned by an Elyria patrolman), there were about seventy-five people, three television crews and a dozen reporters and photographers surrounding the garage. Some people were waving bananas. Tommy called and explained the situation, and I told him he had to keep that garage door shut and not let anybody in until the monkey was captured and secure.

Tommy told everyone to stand back and stay out, and he proceeded to have a slam-bam-and-drag-out chase with that monkey, trying to take him in. Old Seldom Seen went nuts and just about wrecked the entire garage. When Tommy came out with the monkey after almost an hour and a half, he looked like he'd rassled a grizzly.

Tommy told me later that the man had just rearranged his garage—nails and screws in little jars and all that. The monkey overturned every single item in the entire place, and it looked like a hurricane had been through there when they were finished.

I didn't want to deprive Tommy and the staff of their deserved credit, but I wanted that monkey back home. I told him to hurry with the pictures and interviews, just bring Senior back. As prearranged, Tommy called me from a pay phone when he and the monkey were ten minutes from the zoo. I was standing at the front gate with the media when they arrived.

So Tommy drove the zoo truck up and the cameras were rolling. He opened the back of the truck and I saw Seldom Seen Senior glaring up at me with this mean look.

"Now listen up," I told that monkey, pointing my finger

at him. "You've cost us a lot of man-hours, a lot of sleep and a lot of paperwork. You've embarrassed me personally. Now you're back and you ain't goin' nowhere. Don't you ever try that again."

That monkey just looked at me and then, the last thing, he grabbed on to the bars of the cage and started shaking it, screaming like crazy.

"Tommy," I said, feeling more like a jail warden than a zoo director, "take him away." He went screaming and kicking.

We still have those monkeys. They may not have their moat anymore, but they each have about eight wives, so they don't have such a bad life. Makes you wonder why they ever wanted to escape in the first place. Every time I walk by the exhibit, Senior looks at me with that same mean look. I think he hates me to this day, and I'm not sure why. After all, he would never have found a Mrs. Seldom Seen in Cleveland!

∧∧

One of the things I found exasperating in my first year at Columbus was that zoos rarely worked together. There was a very competitive atmosphere in the zoo community at the time, and, to a lesser extent, there still is. Zoos were remodeling natural habitats, raising funds and doing all kinds of new things, but giving or getting advice or sharing information didn't happen that often among zoo directors. What's sad is that the animals are the losers in the long run.

As I mentioned earlier, the Columbus Zoo was behind in the zoo field in the late 1970s. Now, I know everybody has his own place to run and I'm not saying the entire zoo community should have bent over backward to help little old Jack Hanna, but all zoos could have benefited more in the past by working together. Certainly we could have. I'm talking about calling somebody up and saying, "Joe, we're putting in a pond for our snow monkeys . . . any ideas?"

Edward Maruska, director of the Cincinnati Zoo, is one man whom I've never been able to understand or really get to know on a personal basis. He runs one of this country's greatest zoos. I'm very thankful to be able to say that our relationship survived a strange incident back in 1980. Few people would have been as understanding as he was.

On a hot August morning, I heard a panicky call over my walkie-talkie—which I left on all the time—from security to the cheetah pen. (People laughed at me the way I left that walkie-talkie on twenty-four hours a day, but I was proud to have it, proud to be "Unit One," my code number. Listening in kept me informed of everything going on at the zoo, from a busted boiler to a late-night visit from our head veterinarian Dr. Gardner, and I think the employees valued that.)

Anyway, on this particular morning, I was in my office when I realized, hearing the sirens in the background over the radio, that there was an emergency involving the cheetahs. I rushed over and got there just in time to learn that one of our employees had five minutes earlier fed a valuable goose to the cheetahs. I was dumbfounded. How? Why?

The story is weird and a bit complex, and it was tough to get details, but the undeniable bottom line was that a zoo employee who worked in maintenance had purposely fed a rare goose to the cheetahs. To make things worse, this goose was on a breeding loan and belonged to the Cincinnati Zoo.

As I found out later, the woman, I'll call her Jane, was deathly afraid of birds. This, together with the goose's nasty disposition—he liked to bite people—made for a bad match. One of Jane's duties was to clean the bathrooms next to the holding pen for birds, and on this day someone had left the goose in the pen—on purpose or not, I don't know. The bird-house people knew that the goose wasn't supposed to be in that area because it assaulted people.

Predictably, the goose bit Jane while she was cleaning, leaving a welt on her leg. Crying and upset, she ran over to her husband's office—he was head of maintenance—to tell

The cereopsis goose that paid a high price for biting his keeper. (Earl W. Smith III)

him what happened. In his account, he told me later that he was busy with some other people and underestimated how upset she was. "Go feed it to the chee-tahs," were his words, never looking up from his desk, never thinking his wife would take him literally. He was only kidding and trying to dismiss her, which was a big mistake considering how distraught she was.

Jane huffed out madder than ever. She went back over to the bird house, and with the help of a seasonal employee, managed to corral the goose and stuff it into a big garbage container. Now, this other worker was either intimidated, or didn't realize at first what she was up to, or couldn't stop her by himself, whatever. At some point, he ran back to maintenance to tell her husband what was happening, and that's when I heard the call come over the walkie-talkie.

Our security chief, Dave Bricker, zipped over to the cheetah pen with his sirens going full blast. He arrived too late, just as Jane was lifting the garbage container up over the fence, sending the goose to its certain death. The goose never knew what hit him, which was a cheetah going about fifty miles an hour. The cat hit that goose like a bombshell and broke its neck instantly. The cat had no interest in eating it, and the dead goose was just lying on the ground when I got there.

After talking with everybody involved—naturally I wanted to know immediately just what had happened—I went back to my office and sat there, not knowing what to do. I was convinced the goose was on the endangered species list and thought maybe the woman could go to jail for what she'd done. It was that serious.

Then there was Maruska and the Cincinnati Zoo. Here I was, new kid on the block in the zoo world, trying to win the respect of people like him. The man was noted for being tough. Now I had to call him and explain what happened. Didn't I have control of my employees? Didn't they value wildlife? I went home, jogged a couple of miles, and thought about it all night.

A curator came into my office first thing in the morning to tell me that this species of goose had been taken off the endangered list two weeks earlier, which was some relief for both myself and Jane.

"Mr. Maruska? This is Jack Hanna."

"How are you doing?" he asked. "How's the zoo going?"

"Fine," I said, and not much more. "Mr. Maruska, I've got to tell you something. I don't really know how to tell you—this story's incredible. Your cereopsis goose is dead," I said.

"How did it die?" These things happen with zoo exchanges, and he didn't seem overly upset.

"One of my maintenance people fed it to the cheetahs." I blurted that right out at first, but I should have begun with the whole story, which I then rambled into. "It's a long story . . . she's deathly afraid of birds . . . her husband was busy . . . the goose bit her . . ."

"What?" He cut me short. "Slow down, please."

I went on blurting out the story, making very little sense, before he cut me off again.

"Listen, just put this in writing, okay? Just write in a letter what happened. Do that. Thank you."

"I'm sorry," I said to him. "I'm really sorry—I'll make it up to you. I'll get another one. I'll . . ."

At this point I didn't know what to say at all. Fortunately, Maruska knew that incidents like this, if prolonged, hurt everyone, and he considered the case closed once he received the written report. Of course, we also paid for the bird, or I should say, the zoo workers paid for the bird.

Looking back on it, I'm very happy that I did make one right decision and that was not to fire anybody involved with this whole thing. It's too easy to fire people. Jane was suspended for two weeks without pay, and both she and her husband wrote letters of apology before coming back. They continued working for the zoo without incident for several more years.

The paper broke the story, on the front page, with the headline "Columbus Cheetahed Cincinnati on Goose," and this upset me. I hadn't even told the trustees yet, I hadn't told anybody. The Cincinnati Zoo had been very forgiving under the circumstances, and I just thought this was terribly negative publicity. I was so rattled, I called Mel Dodge. Mel surprised me with his reaction.

"Jack, that's the funniest thing I've ever read. I'm still laughing." He was, too. He could barely contain himself.

"Mel, it's not funny," I said, dead serious. "I'm in trouble, I have no respect in the zoo world, I don't have anything."

"Hey, mistakes happen," he told me. "You can't control what other people do."

As usual, I felt better after talking to Mel. He helped me get a grip on things, and though I didn't see the humor in the situation that he did, I got over my self-doubts.

A postscript to the story also appeared in the news in the form of a clever little ditty penned by State Senator Stanley Aronoff (R-Cincinnati)—I didn't think this was funny either. The following limerick was introduced in the Senate as part of a lighthearted resolution to "forbid any further wisequacks about the goose that didn't duck quickly enough":

> There once was a goose out on loan
> Whose form was picked clean to the bone
> When goose-pecked zoo feeders
> Threw it in to the cheetahs
> Where it vanished with nary a moan

One interesting result of this whole affair was that we had a huge crowd that weekend to see the cheetah that killed the goose. Of course, we didn't promote it that way, but that's the power of the media, and that's the way it worked out. This was a classic example of Murphy's Law: if something can go wrong, it will.

(Delaware Gazette)

7

TO
THE
RESCUE

Over the long haul, things don't continue to happen totally by accident, I'm convinced of that. If the trend of my getting calls for animal rescues followed me from Florida to Ohio, well, I guess I may have promoted that somewhat. Like most people, I like to help animals, and if this generates publicity that helps the Columbus Zoo or increases the appreciation and better care of wildlife or house pets—so much the better.

The one that really got me started, the first of my many animal rescues in Columbus, happened in the fall of 1979, my second year at the zoo. As so often happens with these things, it was after dark and I was dog-tired and ready for bed when the doorbell rang. At the door stood a very panicked lady. She introduced herself as Charlotte Stukey from Citizens for Humane Action.

"Mr. Hanna, you've got to come help me," she said. "Someone has thrown a kitten over the O'Shaughnessy Dam."

The O'Shaughnessy Dam lies on the Scioto River next to the zoo. It's not exactly Hoover Dam or Niagara Falls, but it's a scary drop when you look down over the dam from the bridge. It's more than a hundred feet down, and it's safe to say that a human being wouldn't survive such a fall.

"Well, you can forget it, ma'am," I remember telling her right off. "It's dead, probably drowned. You've looked down at that dam, right?"

"No, it's not dead," she insisted. "This cat is stuck on a concrete ledge, ninety feet down from the bridge, right above the turmoil. Please, get in your car and just come look. No one will believe me."

"Why did you come to me?" I asked her.

"The Humane Society is closed and the police and fire departments are too busy. No one will help me. Please come." She told me later that she and her family had spotted the cat while sightseeing at the dam.

I drove over with her to the middle of the dam. I stopped the car and got out with my high-beam flashlight. It was pitch dark out, and I thought this woman was out of her mind.

"It's down there," she said, pointing toward the roaring water.

"Down where?" All I could see was rushing water.

After poking around with the flashlight for a while, I came across this little black form, way down at the bottom, dangerously perched on the ledge of a concrete slab that was maybe two feet wide. From where I was, I could just make out its faint meow.

How it wound up there is beyond comprehension. Talk about a cat with nine lives. Somebody had probably just driven by and flung it out the window, and somehow the kitten had slid down the concrete piling and managed to catch on to the ledge. I couldn't believe it.

I told Mrs. Stukey that it was too dark—I'd come back with help and a rowboat at daylight. I knew there was no way we could do anything at night, and I knew that cat wasn't going anywhere.

The amazing thing was that someone had to be walking across that dam and looking down from the perfect spot just to see that poor little thing. That cat could have stayed there for weeks without anybody spotting it—for all I knew, it had been there two, three days. I didn't know what I was going to do, but I said I'd get a boat and we'd get him tomorrow. Sure. I didn't even have a boat—I barely had a net.

First thing the next morning, I called Mike July, our animal curator. He was the perfect guy to help—he cares a lot for animals, although he'd probably rather sleep than do anything else. Mike's the opposite of me—he loves his sleep.

The two of us went and borrowed a boat from Art the aquarium man, got us a net and went out under that dam about the same time people were driving to work. We didn't call the media, but before we knew it, we had a crowd watching us trying to get the cat.

Our net wouldn't quite reach the ledge, which was about twelve feet over our heads. After flailing around for a while, I realized we were stuck in a turmoil and couldn't maneuver

The O'Shaughnessy Dam. The kitten miraculously landed on the ledge between the spillways some seventy feet below the bridge. (Columbus Zoo file)

The kitten gets knocked into the net...
(Delaware Gazette)

Safe! (Delaware Gazette)

the boat. Now I'm thinking we're in this place forever—the water was swirling, and it scared the hell out of me.

John Becker, zoo operations manager, was up top over the dam, and he came up with an idea to dangle some rope down to scare the cat into our net. That didn't work—it was hard enough getting that long a piece of rope anywhere near the cat. We were even throwing little rocks at it, trying to get it off that ledge. But this wasn't very good either, since they might force the cat off the wrong way, and if the cat went into the rapid water, it was all over. Besides, our aim was terrible.

Then Becker came up with another idea, which was to go get some water balloons and throw them at the cat. It was now two outs, bottom of the ninth, and a three-and-two count on the cat. Becker threw a half dozen of those water balloons, and most of them hit us, not the cat. I was trying to hold the boat in place, Mike had the net. We're getting splattered and I'm thinking it's hopeless, when all of a sudden a water balloon hits that cat flush and knocks it right into the center of our net. The crowd up on the bridge went nuts. By the time another boat came to pull us out of there, people were still clapping and cheering.

The cat wound up in the home of a secretary who worked for WBNS-TV in downtown Columbus. I was honored that she named the cat Hanna, but I wasn't surprised when she told me it was the feistiest cat she'd ever seen. After two years she had to get rid of it, since it never stayed home.

Rescuing one little pussycat from drowning may not seem like such a big deal, but it set a certain precedent around our zoo. The whole thing got heavy coverage in the newspapers, and it established Jack Hanna not just as a zoo director but as a caring person whom people could call on twenty-four hours a day—and that's what people started doing, for better or worse. At the same time, it was good for the Columbus Zoo, because it seemed as though overnight we—and I'm talking about the entire staff—became "people who cared."

∧∧

One of my great misadventures, actually a nonrescue, occurred on a cool, late-fall Sunday night when my brother had come to visit from Knoxville. I was in no way responsible for what happened, but when it was all over, I had to wonder whether or not it was worth it to be a public figure. I also had to wonder how people can do such idiotic things.

My brother Bush had gotten sick of following me around all weekend. (Depending on attendance, weekends can be my busiest time at the zoo. Usually I'll spend all of Saturday and most of Sunday there.) He had come up to see me and the family, and I really hadn't given him too much of my time. By the time Sunday evening rolled around, Bush was just looking forward to a nice dinner at home with Suzi and the kids and a quick trip back home. We had just had a drink and I was putting the steaks on the grill when the phone rang.

"Mr. Hanna?"

"Yes?"

"This is the Columbus police dispatcher. We've received a report that a hippo is loose in the river in downtown Columbus and . . ."

"Yeah, right, and I got the tooth fairy up on my roof talking to Santa Claus right now. See you later," I said, and hung up. Usually I'm not that way, but I was trying to unwind when that call came in and I wasn't in the mood for any jokes.

Less than a minute later the phone rang again, and this time it was the sheriff's department.

"Mr. Hanna, there's a hippo loose in downtown Columbus, and we wondered if you knew anything."

"Wait a minute," I said. "This is for real, isn't it?"

They assured me it was, and wanted to know if I knew anything about it. I didn't. Whoever I was talking to didn't really know much either. I probably should have left this thing alone, but now I was curious. I went out and told Bush, and he looked at me like I was either nuts or drunk.

I immediately called Dave Bricker, my security chief. At

that time, his job at the zoo fell under the city police department. I asked Dave what the heck was going on.

"I just talked to the chief on duty," he told me. "Jack, they've got four squad cars up there, they've got a SWAT team helicopter up there, they've got everybody up there chasing this hippo."

"Did you check our hippos?" I asked him. "See how many we've got there."

"I just did that, Jack. They're all there. I counted three: Pete, Mama and the baby."

"Well, that's how many we had yesterday and how many we've always had. Where do you suppose *this* hippo came from?"

"Jack, I don't know. I'm not *supposed* to know where the hippo came from." Boy oh boy, I sure wasn't getting a lot of information around here. I told Bricker to come pick me up and we'd go downtown and check this out.

I went back out to the porch where Bush was nursing his drink and, just trying to be nice, trying to involve him a little bit, I asked him where he thought the hippo came from.

"Jack, I don't really care," he said. He acted like this was somebody's idea of a bad joke—which, for all I knew, it was. I asked him if he'd take a ride with us to see what was happening.

"I'm staying right here; I've had enough of all this crappy stuff," he told me. "And another thing—I'm never coming to visit you again while you're working."

"Fine," I said. "You don't have to go. But you know I can't shoot very well, and I can't lasso at all." Bricker was bringing along a tranquilizer gun and two sets of ropes. At the mention of shooting and lassoing, being the cow farmer he was, Bush decided to come along.

All right, I'd had a drink, but I still knew there couldn't possibly be a hippo in the Olentangy River in downtown Columbus. Or could there? Anyway, there was a SWAT team on hand—something was going on. A Loch Ness monster from Lake Erie? Something out of the river muck after two thousand years? I didn't want to miss the opportunity to help corral the Ohio Monster or something.

On our way downtown in Bricker's car, we monitored the whole situation over the police radio, and it was apparent from all the cop talk that something serious was going on. About two minutes before we got there, a voice addressed us: "Please have Mr. Hanna ready. We've got the helicopter and chair ready to bring him out over the river with his ropes."

My throat went dry. No way I was going out over that river dangling from a helicopter seat. "Bush, I don't know what it is," I said to my brother, "but you've got to do this for me. You live on a farm, you know how to lasso."

"Okay," he said. "I'll lasso it—I'll shoot it, too." He didn't care; he only half believed this whole thing anyway. He thought we were all crazy, and he wasn't far from wrong.

When we got there, it looked like the President had just arrived or something. There were squad cars, fire trucks, helicopters, spotlights, TV crews, fog lights. I wasn't three steps out of the car when a guy I knew, the head man on the SWAT team, took me aside and said, "Jack, I've got a big problem."

"What's wrong?" I asked him.

"You're not going to believe this," he said, "but we've just found out that it's only a river otter. I don't know who made the mistake."

"What? A hippopotamus weighs at least three thousand pounds, a river otter will go twenty or thirty pounds at the most—how could you guys get the two confused?" He couldn't answer me.

Now I was mad, and the whole thing was flashing before me, like the lights on the cruisers. What was my brother going to think? What about the steaks at home? Why was I (and the zoo) involved? On top of it all, they were asking me to make an announcement to the media, even though they're the ones who screwed up.

Dana Tyler, who's the anchorperson for Channel 10

News in Columbus, was right there, right on top of me, asking, "Jack, what is it? What's going on now?"

"Dana," I said, taking a deep breath—somehow I knew ol' Jack was going to take the rap on this fiasco. "There's obviously been a mistake here. You're not going to believe this, but from what I'm told, it looks like it's a large river otter."

"A what?"

"An otter, a large river otter."

"How much can it weigh?" she asked me.

"Well, in prehistoric times," I said, and here I started making things up, "it could have weighed up to two hundred pounds." Of course, who cares about prehistoric times? This is today. "But today," I said, "a big one might weigh up to twenty pounds." I really wasn't sure about this, but I was doing the best I could.

"But, Dana," I added, digging a deeper hole, "have you ever seen a person swimming—you know how they come up with their back and make the water roll and everything? That otter was swimming, making the water roll in these big waves, and it looked like a hippo."

I was explaining all this on TV and she just shook her head and said, "Jack, what are you doing? I don't believe this. What do *you* think happened?"

"Don't ask me," I said. "I was called from home; you people were here forty-five minutes before I even knew about it." That's what I should have said in the first place. Next thing I knew, she was interviewing Bush, who, of course, had no idea what was going on. Nobody had any clear-cut answers on this thing.

The next day's newspaper ran a story headlined "River Monster Turns Out to Be Otter," and the television coverage of the incident led off the "year in review" news show on New Year's Eve—some kind of funny "Who can forget . . ." sort of thing. My brother Bush never forgot it; he's been back to visit only once since then.

∧∧

One of my busiest Saturdays ever at the zoo—this was a time when I had a lot of speeches and zoo tours to prepare, mostly on Saturdays—I got a call from some guy who was frantic.

"Mr. Hanna," he said, "I've got a big problem, and I don't know who to call. My German shepherd had puppies two days ago and one of them fell down the heating-and-air-conditioning vent in my house." If he really didn't know who to call, how come my phone ends up ringing?

"Can't you reach down in there and get it?" I asked.

"I can't," he said. "I've tried everything. He's way down in there, and I can't get him out."

I wrote down the man's phone number and told him I'd see what I could do. After I hung up, I crumpled the note and threw it in the wastebasket. I had speeches and zoo tours scheduled for that day. I was very busy, and I wanted that note to just go away, but it wouldn't. I didn't want to be bothered with it, but I kept hearing the guy's voice.

Finally, I went back to the wastebasket and found the number, called the guy and told him I'd be out there. He lived about twenty miles away—a real pain in the butt.

So I went out there with Bricker, also Glenn Baker, a real character who's been with the zoo forever and works in air conditioning on the side. We pulled up to the house and there was already a group of people gathered—"Hey, Jack Hanna's here," and all that. A kid came up and asked for my autograph—I signed, but I really didn't feel like it, which is not like me at all. Just show me where the dog is.

Captain Dave Bricker, my security chief, with a lion cub. (Jack Hanna)

The house was about twenty-five or thirty years old—nothing fancy by any means, just a nice little white house.

The man showed me the vent, and I got up next to it and listened real close. I could hear little puppy sounds.

"Well, let's get a saw," I said, "and we'll cut a hole in the floor."

"It's poured concrete," the guy said.

I couldn't believe it; I didn't think they made houses like that. We pulled a little of the carpet back, and sure enough, the metal vent was centered into poured concrete, a foot thick, with no basement either. No crawl space, nothing. The vents went through that concrete to the heating-and-air-conditioning system about thirty feet away.

Baker knew air conditioning, so I figured he could take care of this. He stuck his arm in there, but of course he couldn't reach the dog. We tried a sewer snake, monkeying it this way and that, but the puppy wasn't moving—had to be fifteen feet down. This was Glenn's first rescue call, by the way, and he was having a ball. He wasn't just going to rescue the dog, he was going to rescue the world, Baker was. I just wanted to get back to the zoo.

"Tell you what," Baker told the dog owner. "We're gonna pull up some more of that carpet and we're gonna take us a hammer and chisel and take up some of that concrete down where we think that dog is."

The guy didn't mind, he just wanted his puppy back. So we pulled up about ten feet of glued rug, pretty well ruining it, and we hammered and bored a hole down through the concrete into the vent. Now we heard the dog yipping a lot better, but we still couldn't reach him—he'd moved farther back.

"Aw, geez," I said. "Just cancel my whole day." It was now two hours since I'd gotten that call and we weren't any closer to the dog than when we got there.

"I got an idea," said Baker. "Bricker, why don't you go out to your police cruiser and call the Sewers and Drains Department, have them bring one of their jackhammers over."

Baker's idea seemed all right, like one I'd think of myself.

Whoever showed up, I'd take care of them with a load of free zoo passes. A half hour later, the Sewers Department truck pulled up with a guy and his jackhammer. He said it was a slow day and didn't mind coming over—he was probably getting double overtime.

So we went into the house, got that jackhammer going, and it was something. Everybody had to go outside. Within thirty seconds there was so much dust, you couldn't see a foot in front of your face.

"Whoa!" I yelled at the top of my lungs. "Stop! Stop! This is terrible, we're destroying your house," I told the guy. Not to mention that his puppy might be vibrating to death.

"This isn't my house," said the guy, dropping the bombshell. "I'm renting it."

"You're what? You're kidding me, right?"

Baker started laughing. "You're kidding this man, aren't you?" he said.

"No, I don't own it. I rent it," the guy repeated.

"I don't believe this is happening," said Bricker. Up till now, he'd just been standing by. Again, Bricker, my security chief, worked for me and the zoo, but he was officially on the police force and this was hardly official conduct.

"Didn't you call the landlord and tell him what we're doing?" I asked the guy.

"No, I didn't call him. I don't ever talk to the guy," he said.

"You told me I could tear up your carpet, tear up your floor. There's got to be over two thousand dollars' worth of damage here." I was steamed. Baker was still laughing, and Bricker looked sick—and I could wind up paying for this crap.

"Now listen," I told the guy. "We're going to get your puppy, but I want you to sign a piece of paper saying we're not responsible for this mess. Somebody's going to sign something, because I'm not paying for your house."

Well, we blasted that floor another three minutes or so, and the jackhammer noise made the puppy back up all the way into the air conditioning unit. Baker heard him in there and pulled him out, and he was all of a sudden a big hero, which was fine with me.

We left the place a shambles, carpet and concrete lying all over the place. Baker didn't even put the guy's air conditioner back together. He just left it on the floor since I had to get back to the zoo. That landlord still probably doesn't know what happened to his house, but no one ever called me.

When I get phone calls from various city departments, I try to give them as much attention as possible. As I've said over and over, the Columbus Zoo owes a debt to the entire community, and it's important that we all work together. Some departments I've never heard from and never will, and some come at me out of the blue—like the Water Department.

On one of those rare mild early spring days, I got a call, about five years back, from an official at the Water Department. He told me that one of his meter readers had reported an encounter with a large alligator at a residence near the fairgrounds. The department head asked me to check it out. As it stood, his worker was frightened and refused to return to the neighborhood. It was a busy Friday. I didn't believe the story and didn't want to go, but the man was politely begging me to go down there.

I called Bricker to come along since this area of town is tough. It's not the kind of place where you can walk up, knock on a door by yourself and say, "Excuse me, but I want to see your twelve-foot alligator." I would have called these people first, but they didn't have a phone.

Bricker didn't want to get a search warrant, and I agreed with him. A lot of times, people who have exotic animals don't know what the law is and could get in a lot of trouble. If I can talk to them and possibly get the animal to a zoo or a proper home without going through all the legal stuff—I'd rather do that.

So Bricker and I went down to this address, a little house near the Ohio State Fairgrounds. An older man came to the door and asked what we wanted. He wasn't impolite but not overly friendly either.

"Jack Hanna, from the zoo," I said, putting out my hand. The guy ignored it and just looked at us. "We had a report of an alligator here."

Bricker was wearing his police uniform, and I know this helped. If it'd just been me, the guy would have lied to me, would have told me a story. Anyway, he called back in the house and said, "Son, they're here to see your alligator." Just like that.

A man appeared, about thirty years old, and very nervous. "Nothing's wrong with my alligator," he said.

"Look," I said. "We're not going to hurt your alligator—all we want to do is see him. We got a report the water meter man stepped on a twelve-foot alligator."

"Okay—if you won't take him away from me."

"I won't take him away from you." I thought the guy was going to break down. Bricker thought the guy probably had a two-foot pet alligator that he'd brought up from Florida a couple years ago or something.

"All right, then," he said. "We'll go see Allie." He took us around the side of the house to a basement door and called down. "Here, Allie. Here, Allie."

It was the most incredible thing. Up the stairs came this ten- or twelve-foot, 250- to 300-pound alligator!

Bricker and I both jumped back scared to death.

"He ain't gonna hurt you," the guy said. Then he patted the alligator on the head and said, "Come on, Allie. Let's go outside."

The alligator walked up those basement steps—so help me—went out in the back yard and lay down in the sun.

"This is where it happened," said the son. "I had Allie out—I was sunning him—and I went inside the house for a minute. The man must have come across the fence and stepped on him. But Allie wouldn't hurt him."

Dancing with Allie, the 250-pound house pet. (Michael W. Pogany)

"Maybe not," I said, "but that thing could eat a hundred-pound boy. How long have you had him?"

"Fourteen years."

Fourteen years. This guy had an alligator near downtown Columbus ever since he was a kid. You used to be able to buy them in Florida; now you can't, ever since they went on the endangered list—actually they're on the "threatened" list today. He bought it when it was a foot long and kept it. What amazed me was the care he provided it—most of those "pet" alligators died from people not knowing how to care for them.

"What do you feed Allie?" I asked him.

"Rabbits," he said. He took us to the back of the yard and showed us these cages with about thirty rabbits in them. He said the neighbors thought he raised rabbits, and as far as he knew, they didn't know he had an alligator.

Then the kid—I'm calling him a kid; he was a little slow-witted, he seemed so young—showed us pictures of him and Allie taking showers and baths together. He was actually lying down in the water with this alligator.

"Allie just loves it when I take a bath with him," he said. Bricker sat there, mouth open, shaking his head. We'd been out on some crazy calls, but I'd never seen him so dumbfounded.

Now, I had a problem here. I was impressed with this guy's care for his alligator. I was probably wrong, and it goes against my general beliefs about people owning exotic animals, but I wanted the guy to keep his alligator. Bricker and I went outside to talk it over.

"What are we going to do?" I asked Bricker. "I don't want to take that alligator."

"Yeah, but he's breaking the law," he said.

"I know, but let's wait until somebody officially calls us to go pick up an alligator. I really don't need any more gators at the zoo anyway."

"Okay," said Bricker. "Let's act like we never saw it."

"What about the water man? What do we tell him?" I asked.

"Tell him whatever you want," he said. "I didn't see an alligator, did you?"

So we left father, son and Allie back there. When I got back to the office, I called the water man and did some fast double-talking.

"I'm not saying your meter man didn't step on an alligator," I told him. "All I'm saying is we went around that area and didn't see one."

Of course, I kept real quiet on this one and didn't call any papers or anything. But the funny thing is, a few years later, Allie and owner were in the *National Enquirer* together—the story of a man and his alligator in an urban setting. I recognized him immediately. I guess a lot of people probably thought it was bunk since it was in the *National Enquirer,* but I knew better.

*M*ike Goode, Dan Badgley and I hold the giant seventeen-foot python that later scared the heck out of David Letterman. (Columbus Zoo, Earl W. Smith III)

8

SNAKES

Of all the animal world, snakes are probably the most hated, ill-regarded, misunderstood beasts there are. I've found that people are generally deathly afraid of any kind of snake. Forget the fact that most snakes are hardly more harmful to humans than a housefly—let's face it, they're victims of a bum rap that goes all the way back to Adam and Eve.

Sometimes, when I give a speech, I'll pick a lady from the audience to come up to the podium, and I'll have her close her eyes. When she opens them, my assistants will be holding a snake, semi-wrapped around her. Of course, she'll be repulsed or shocked and this gets a big reaction from the audience. But the way I choose my "victim" usually depends on what kind of belt she, or he, is wearing—like snakeskin, you get my point? I'll say something like "You don't like this live thing squirming near you, but you don't mind wearing his dead cousin around your waist, do you?"

Knowing how David Letterman hates snakes, I don't try to get him to hold them, like I do with other animals on the show. Once, I appeared on *Late Night* with the largest python I've ever seen—it weighed about 170 pounds, was seventeen feet long and took three of us to hold it up. Dave stood all the way across the set and turned nearly bleach white before we got that thing off.

I personally like snakes, but I respect them, too. I have to, given the kind I'm dealing with most of the time. A spitting cobra can blind you in a split second; a bite from a coral snake can be deadly. I've learned a lot about snakes from Dr. Joe Cross, a reptile expert as well as my personal doctor, who has treated me for everything from minor bites to mental stress resulting from this crazy business.

I also don't mind people owning snakes, even poisonous ones, provided they know how to take care of them and are cautious toward the general public. Unfortunately, this is all too often the exception. That's when somebody can get hurt: either the owner, an innocent bystander, or an innocent snake. And that's when I usually get a phone call.

∧∧

On a beautiful autumn late afternoon, back in 1984, I was just getting ready to leave the zoo when I received a phone call from the Columbus chief of police.

"Jack," he said, "we've got a little problem with some snakes in an apartment down on the Ohio State campus. Can you come down and help us out?"

"Yeah, I know—this kind of call comes in all the time," I told him, trying to cut him off, "but I'm real busy, and I can't get down there right now." I was meeting Don Malenick, the president of Worthington Industries, for a drink. It was his company that had given us money to remodel the gorilla exhibit, my first large donation, and they had remained one of our steadiest contributors.

"Well, all right," he said, "but if you could get down there later—these are poisonous snakes, mostly cobras and . . ."

"Cobras?"

That got my attention. The chief went on to tell me that a neighbor had noticed a terrible odor coming through the vents for over two weeks and had called the landlord. The landlord had gone into the apartment, seen the snakes and called the cops. I was concerned because cobras can be deadly, and that smell probably meant mistreated animals.

The chief told me he could send a cruiser right away to

pick me up, so I said all right. I called Don and asked if he would mind coming along to look at some snakes before we had that drink. He said fine and was tickled when we pulled up to his house with the police car.

I could tell, as Don got into the back of the car behind the screen, that he enjoyed this kind of thing cropping up. He's a rugged individual and runs a large company, but maybe this was a change from his daily coat-and-tie world. Me, I just wanted to get away from the animal world and go have a drink. Don was ready for whatever came up.

So we drove down to this typical university apartment complex—a group of buildings with duplexes. There were already four squad cars on hand in one of the parking areas, one with its lights flashing. The captain walked over and introduced himself.

"Jack, I appreciate your coming down. We've got a real problem here," he said. "There are over fifty snakes in this house."

"Did you go in and count fifty snakes?" I asked him. I didn't mean to be a wise guy, but people always seem to exaggerate and get alarmed when it comes to snakes.

"No," he said, "but I walked in the front room there and this guy's got spiders on his mantel and it's dark in there and it's plenty weird. We have him under arrest now."

So now we're into spiders. I couldn't help thinking that this whole thing was a joke, except for the poor guy under arrest.

"What have you got here, a cult or something?" I asked the captain.

"None of my men want to go upstairs into the guy's bedroom. One of them got halfway up, saw this cobra on the bed and came back down."

I remember thinking then that it was stupid not to have my reptile people along. They handle snakes all day long. I hadn't considered it that big a deal, maybe one or two snakes. But what if I was wrong? I know a little bit about snakes, but I wasn't really ready to handle a poisonous one.

So we went into the apartment, which was in semi-darkness. The lights didn't work—the electricity had probably been turned off. There was still some daylight left, but curtains or sheets had been nailed to the walls over the windows. The stench was overpowering, beyond anything I'd ever experienced, and I've been around a lot of animal shit in my life.

Sitting on a couch, just as we entered, was the snake owner and a policeman. Roy Dulin was the snake owner's name, and he was something else. In the dim light, I could just make out the long dark wig he was wearing, pulled back from his shoulders in a ponytail. He was in his early thirties, wore metal-rimmed glasses and had a faraway, stoned-out look in his eyes.

On the mantel were live tarantulas in little boxes. Don and I looked at each other and didn't say anything.

"Upstairs, that's where the snakes are," said the policeman.

"Well, why don't you have him go up there?" I said, pointing to Roy. "They're his snakes."

"Nooo, nooo," said Roy, shaking his head. He wasn't about to help—he was in a trance.

The policeman handed me his flashlight, motioning me to go first.

"Don, you want to go with me?" My buddy Don—I don't know why I asked him. Maybe I was getting the willies myself.

"Sure," said Don, cheerful as hell. "But I'm not going to touch any snakes."

So we proceeded up the stairs, and I nudged open the bedroom door. On the bed was an aquarium tank with just a piece of cloth over it, and in it was a six-foot-long cobra—that's the first thing I saw. As my eyes got accustomed to the dark, I realized that there were actually three Egyptian cobras hooding up in that fish tank with just a flimsy sheet as a cover. If they wanted to get out, no problem.

"I don't believe this." That's all I said.

*T*he main gate at the Columbus Zoo. Over nine hundred thousand visitors pass through here yearly. (Columbus Zoo, Nancy Staley)

Teak and Amber.
(Columbus Zoo, Nancy Staley)

*F*our Bengal tiger cubs. They don't get much cuter than this.
(Columbus Zoo, Nancy Staley)

Suzi and Taj.
(Columbus Zoo, Rick Prebeg)

*M*adagascar cockroaches make good portable pets. Not everybody likes them as much as I do. (Karen Kuehn)

*R*are Chinese golden monkeys, an exchange gift from China.
(Columbus Zoo, Nancy Staley)

*R*oscoe rides in his Radio Flyer.
(Marsha King)

*T*here are many moments of great natural beauty at the zoo.
(Columbus Zoo, Rick Preburg)

*O*ne of Crazy Roy's cobras. (Columbus Zoo, Nancy Staley)

Behind me, the cop looked back and said, "Jack doesn't believe this." Then there was another cop behind Don who said, "Jack doesn't believe this." It was like the Three Stooges—the word went on down the stairs and out the door to the rest of the police.

"I can't believe they don't get out," I said.

"They're not going to get out," said Roy—he had heard me from downstairs—"because they're my friends."

As I looked around the room, I realized Roy had a lot of "friends." In another container on the floor were two rattlers, both overfed. One was easily six feet long and had to weigh ten pounds. There was a garbage can in the corner with a nine-foot python in it that weighed over sixty pounds. In a chest, in the drawers where most people keep shirts, he had three copperheads. In another aquarium he had a boom-slang, a dangerous African tree snake.

It was mind-boggling. Here were about twenty snakes in this little bedroom, all poisonous, all deadly poisonous except for the python, which probably could swallow a medium-sized dog. The guy couldn't possibly sleep in here. It was like the pit in *Raiders of the Lost Ark*, or worse. Just call me Ohio Jones.

Surprisingly, the snakes were in good condition, though some were overweight (this was confirmed later by my reptile people). For feeding his collection, Roy had live rats and mice all over the place, which added to the smell. He worked at an animal research lab, which is probably where he got his snake feed, although he claimed he bought them. There was also a thirty-gallon container half filled with chirping crickets, for feeding his spiders.

It took Don and me a few minutes to settle down and regain our senses, but after that, I literally got the chills—I didn't want to be there. It was pretty creepy, but we couldn't just leave. The police wanted the snakes out.

"Roy," I yelled down. "Come up here."

"They won't hurt you," he said.

"Get him up here," I told the officers. "We're not touching these snakes."

Roy came up, and I was relieved to see that he had a snake hook. We had to somehow gather these things up and get them out of the apartment safely. I had the cops get me some silver duct tape, and Don and I started taping down whatever covers were on the containers, while Roy moved the snakes as we told him to. Some of those aquariums had cracked glass or holes in them, and we had to tape those, too. The other snakes were transferred to garbage cans that Don and I had borrowed around the area.

I'll say this about Roy: he knew and loved his snakes. He would just reach in and pluck a cobra up by hand. He knew how to do this just like the professional people I knew who worked with snakes all day long. We packed the snakes up as best we could, and once I felt they were secure, we moved them down to the parking lot next to the apartments.

Roy had handled the snakes to pack them up, but he wouldn't help us move them; he was kind of upset we were in his house and bothering his snakes. It was already decided they were going to the zoo. I kept wishing Herbie the herpetologist was here. He would have had a ball with this guy.

We had all the snakes assembled and ready to go, but I'd neglected to put the lid down tight on the big python. The lid fell off and he got partway out and the cops were screaming all over the place. I thought this was sort of funny; that was the one snake that didn't worry me—he was nonvenomous and well fed. We just shoved him back in and waited for the paddy wagon.

The paddy wagon showed up with a policewoman behind the wheel, but she refused to take this cargo. No way.

"I'll drive drunks, rapists and murderers," she told the captain, "but I won't drive these snakes."

So they got a substitute driver. Meanwhile, I had called the home of Dan Badgley, our head reptile keeper, and told him to meet me at the zoo. It was almost ten o'clock.

"What are you doin', Jack?" Dan asked me.

"I'm bringing a bunch of snakes up there."

"We don't need any more snakes."

"Look," I said, "we get our money from the city, and the police asked me to take the snakes. Who else is going to take them?" Dan's a good guy and all, but I really wasn't in the mood to discuss all this.

So we get the snakes all in—Don and I are with them in the back of the paddy wagon; Roy's in a police car. We hadn't gone a hundred yards when Don looked up in that cool, calm way of his and said, "Whoa, Jack, those copperheads are getting out."

I jumped up and looked back at the box, and son of a

gun if those damn copperheads hadn't pushed the top off. Copperheads are very aggressive snakes, and I didn't want to be bitten. Don was laughing.

"Don, this ain't no bullshit," I said. "Get the driver to stop."

Don banged on the glass and yelled, "A snake's out." The driver slammed on the brakes and that knocked about six of those snakes out of their boxes and onto the floor of the wagon. I tried to get us out the back door of the paddy wagon, but the damn thing locked from the outside so that prisoners couldn't get out. When the policewoman came to unlock it, I was pushing on the door so hard she couldn't get it open.

"Quit pushing," Don told me.

I eased up, the door opened and I went flying out. I was getting a little panicky—this whole scene was getting ridiculous.

"Everybody calm down," Roy was now telling us in this real weird voice. "Everybody calm down. I'll catch the snakes."

He reached inside the wagon and casually picked up a copperhead by the tail and held it upside down. "See?" he said. "It's not going to hurt anybody."

I ran back to the apartment for the snake hook and had Roy round up the ones that were flipping around on the floor of the wagon. We repacked and resealed the crates, containers and what not. Now we got all loaded up again— Roy rode alone in the paddy wagon with his snakes this time, while Don and I rode in the police car. We finally got to the zoo around eleven o'clock that night.

Before going home, Don and I decided to have one drink. I got home around midnight and took off all my dirty, smelly clothes at the front door. Stark naked, I walked into the kitchen. There stood my wife, Suzi.

"Have you been drinking?" she asked me.

"Suzi," I said, "you are not going to believe this. I've only had one drink. I captured twenty-two snakes. You'll read about it in the paper tomorrow."

"You did what?"

"Smell my clothes if you don't believe me. I'll tell you about it tomorrow; I'm going to bed."

Well, Suzi saw the dirty clothes, but I suspect that she believed me anyway. She knows me well enough to expect anything by now. I went to bed and dreamt about snakes.

Roy went to court to try to get his snakes back, but the judge wouldn't go for it. I actually felt sorry for the guy in court; he looked like he was going to cry—he really loved those snakes. "I don't want to hurt anybody," I remember him saying. "I just want my snakes."

The paddywagon filled with dozens of Roy's tacky poisonous snakes.
(*Columbus Citizen Journal*)

*D*an Badgley and a rhino iguana. (Columbus Zoo, Rick Prebeg)

We kept the cobras and traded the others. I don't think we ever made a dime off Roy's collection, even if it was one of the most extensive and expensive I had ever seen. Dan Badgley has bred those cobras twice, and I'm pleased to say that at last count some thirty-two eggs have been hatched. So old crazy Roy has a legacy at the Columbus Zoo.

Owners of exotic pets have to understand that some-one—a repairman, anybody—can come on their property and be in serious danger, or that the animals themselves can get loose. What if Roy's cobras had slithered off into the building's air-conditioning vents? I've seen it happen. That apartment building would have been a time bomb.

The snake may only cost ten to twenty dollars—Roy's were worth more—but the proper place to keep the snake should cost over two thousand dollars. Ninety-five percent of the people who buy wild animals at auctions don't have a safe and proper habitat. Roy's bedroom was not the right place for those snakes, no matter how healthy they were or how much he loved them.

∧∧

The year 1984 was a good one for exotic snakes in Columbus, Ohio, at least for our zoo. We kept getting them free, from the community, no less.

A few months before meeting the illustrious Roy Dulin, I got a call one late-spring night from a Franklin County sheriff's deputy. He told me that a man had seen a twelve-foot-long snake crawling around his back porch, that it had brushed up against his leg and scared the daylights out of him. He said the man had a two-year-old daughter and sounded real scared. Would I check it out?

The place wasn't close by, and Suzi and I were about to barbecue some chicken, and it probably wasn't anywhere near a twelve-foot snake, but it was the sheriff calling and he did mention a two-year-old girl, so I bit.

I grabbed a couple of pillowcases and a rake—my little snake-catching kit—and took off in my white Columbus Zoo station wagon. I drove about forty miles, following the directions the man had given me, and pulled up at this nice-looking farmhouse way out in the sticks.

Right off, I noticed a lot of people standing around holding beers; I think they were having a barbecue or picnic, but nobody looked real happy. Everybody was standing around a big metal hog feeder that had a big piece of plywood on top of it with a dozen cinder blocks holding it down. They were all staring at that big bucket looking anxious.

"Thank goodness you're here," said Phil Corbitt, the man who'd called the sheriff. "We just don't know what to do. Maybe there's more of these running around."

"More of what? Where?"

"That thing in there," he said, pointing at the feeder.

"You could keep a gorilla under all those cinder blocks," I told him, trying to lighten things up.

"No, there's a snake in there," he said, dead serious.

"Well, let's take these blocks off and let's see the snake."

Nobody wanted to lift up that cover—I even heard a few people say, "No way." I told them that I couldn't very well transport the hog feeder, whatever was in it and the cinder blocks back to town in the station wagon. Besides, I had my little pillowcases and my rake. Reluctantly, they agreed, after I assured them that we could catch the snake if it escaped again, which was very unlikely.

They lifted up that board, and I thought I was going to drop my teeth—I wanted to put those blocks back on. It was a much bigger snake than anything we had at the zoo. It was a python, about ten to twelve feet long, and had to weigh seventy to eighty pounds, a lot of weight for a snake. It was also in magnificent condition—I don't know how it had lived in the cooler weather at that time of year, but it didn't have a runny nose like some snakes have when they have respiratory problems.

How it had gotten there was a mystery to me since there were no houses within two or three miles. Later on we found out that one of the nearest neighbors who had recently moved away did indeed raise snakes, so that's obviously where it came from. A snake like that does not hatch in the American wild, and that's what worried Phil Corbitt—maybe this thing had left some eggs lying around somewhere? I told him I didn't think so—hell, I didn't know.

Anyway, we put the cover back on, and the folks helped me put the hog feeder into the back of the station wagon. I put four cinder blocks on top so I could rest assured that the snake would be secure for the trip back to the zoo.

About twenty miles up Interstate 270, listening to country music as I always do, I felt something up against my leg. It was the snake. That snake had somehow slithered out of that hog feeder, squeezed itself out—quiet, real quiet—and come up to the front seat.

I shuddered a little, and my heart went down to my stomach, because I didn't know if the snake would bite me. He couldn't kill me—he wasn't poisonous—but I knew that he had a couple hundred teeth shaped like fishhooks. Mother Nature gave him these so that he could hold on to prey. If snakes fight at the zoo, and one latches on to another, we pour hot water on them to relax their muscles. But I didn't have any hot water in the car. If it bit me, I might as well just sit there.

I couldn't get out and handle a snake that big anyway, and besides, I was on the interstate, so I just kept on driving, and I waited to see what the snake would do. For a while, he just lay there against my knee. But after a few minutes that seemed like hours, he started moving again. The damn thing crawled right across my lap—the entire snake—on up over my shoulder and into the back. He just lay down and curled up on top of his big bucket and didn't move the whole drive back.

Suzi and I had a big argument when I got home. I've brought my share of animals home over the years, but this snake was too much. She didn't want it staying around the house, not even locked up in the car.

"What if that thing gets loose and kills a kid up here?"
she said.

"Suzi, that thing ain't going nowhere; it's impossible."

I couldn't unload the snake at the zoo by myself, and it
was now too late to call people in from home to help me,
so he would just have to stay there. Of course, I locked the
car doors, but I must admit, I went out and checked on him
a few times during the night, since I had left the windows
cracked for ventilation. When I came out in the morning,
that snake hadn't moved an inch from the top of the hog
feeder.

Back at the zoo, we put the snake in quarantine for a
week and then put him on special display. You know who
I'd like to see on display? The crazy guy who let that snake
loose in the first place!

∧∧

One summer evening I got a call from a lady who was
frantic. She said that she lived out in the country with three
other women and that there was a snake in her commode.
None of them had dared use the toilet for the last eight
hours and they didn't know what to do. Could I come help?

I told her to go check and see if the snake was still in
there. When she came back and said it was, I said all right,
I'd come out and help her get rid of it.

We turned this into a family affair, with Suzi and the girls
all piling into the station wagon. Of course, I took my
trusty old snake rake and pillowcase. We drove about six
miles into the country up to a very meager little farmhouse
that looked abandoned except for a beautiful, well-cared-
for vegetable garden.

The rickety screen door was open, and as we walked in,
I saw four nervous ladies all sitting on the couch. When I
came in, you'd have thought the Lone Ranger had arrived
from the way they greeted me. They were glad to see Jack
Hanna, the great snake handler. They showed me to the
bathroom, but none of them would go in; in fact, they
stepped back a safe distance. The funny thing is, I'm as
scared of snakes as the next person.

I went into the bathroom and saw that the lid to the commode was shut, with a ten-pound pot lying on top of it. I called Suzi so we could check this out together. I took the pot off, and Suzi, fearless as ever, lifted up the toilet lid. What we found was a big old corn snake, maybe four feet long. It looked quite comfortable, all coiled around in there like an Italian sausage.

I didn't realize it at the time, but that snake had probably come up through the rotted floorboards in the bathroom. A toilet bowl is a cool, enticing place for a snake on a hot summer day.

Suzi used the rake to get the snake out of the toilet and into the bathtub and somehow steered it into the pillowcase I was holding. The girls were watching, giggling and making fake screams the whole time. The snake was harmless, but it looked awfully mean. I wouldn't like to find it in my toilet.

The ladies were ecstatic when we got the snake out of their house. One of them kept trying to give me fifty dollars, which I refused. It was a nice gesture because they were so poor. (One of these days, I just might start charging.) I immediately noticed that the others were all lined up waiting to use the bathroom.

They kept insisting they owed us, so I told them we'd take some vegetables out of the garden I'd noticed as we drove up. They said fine, and we drove home happy with a car full of vegetables and a big snake. The snake we dropped off at the zoo on the way home.

Now, this story's no big deal; the ending isn't all that hot—I know that. But I also know that ever since that day I always take a good look before I sit down on the toilet, especially when I go camping.

∧∧

At the Columbus Zoo, we have one of the finest reptile facilities in the world. It's noted as much for its displays and layout as it is for a reptile breeding program that includes turtles and just about every kind of poisonous and nonpoisonous snake and lizard there.

Our reptile house is a nice place to visit, but I wouldn't want to spend the night in there, which is exactly what accidentally happened to a young couple out on their first date.

The phone rang at six-thirty on the Monday morning after Daylight Savings Time started. George Merritt, our nighttime security man, was calling, and naturally, I knew something was wrong, or he wouldn't be calling at that hour.

"What's up, Merritt?" I asked him.

"There's been a big mistake at the zoo—I don't know how to tell you."

"What mistake?"

"Security . . . uh . . . somebody locked a young couple—college kids—in the reptile house last night. A groundsman found them when he went over there to clean up this morning. They were pretty upset and are at my office now."

"What'd they say when you first saw them?"

"The guy said he wanted to call his boss, the girl asked to use the bathroom, then they asked to see you."

I rushed over to the zoo to meet the two kids because naturally I was concerned for their overall well-being. The couple was very nice about the whole thing—more relieved than they were scared or angry. The boy was hoarse from yelling for help all night and anxious to get to his early-morning job. He had no way of knowing that we have a Honeywell system that controls lighting and temperature automatically. During the night, the lights will go on and off in different exhibits at random and I imagine it can be quite scary. That, combined with the sounds of rattling rattlers and alligators splashing around, was nerve-wracking.

Apparently, the couple had heard the keeper's call at closing time, but they just hadn't been able to get to the door in time. They saw the door closing and yelled, but nobody heard them. This was at six o'clock the previous night.

From a security standpoint, it was embarrassing to me because that's the one animal area security doesn't enter at night. We only check the temperature controls on the outside of the building. The young man had plans for law school, and he told me that that was why he didn't try to break out through the glass entrance. He didn't want a police report, which I was thankful for. The story has a happy ending—the couple got married a year later.

*K*oko, one of the largest Asian bull elephants in captivity, now weighs ten thousand pounds!
(Columbus Zoo, Earl W. Smith III)

9

RISKY BUSINESS

I once met a man at a luncheon who had just been appointed head of insurance regulation for the state of Ohio. "How do you know," he asked me, "that one of your animals isn't going to get out on a busy weekend afternoon and kill somebody?"

The man was kind of arrogant and spoiling for an argument, but he probably never expected an honest answer.

"I don't know that they won't," I told him.

"What? You know that your rates are based on that, don't you?"

"I know all about my rates, pal," I told him. "I just don't know what tomorrow will bring at the zoo any more than I know when a race car will crash or a football player will get a concussion, and neither do you."

The fact is, we take every possible precaution at the zoo to ensure that the public will be safe, and, of course, we can never be too careful. The idea is to try to gauge the strength of animals and at the same time allow the public a decent view. There will always be accidents, especially with keepers, who have the most dangerous of jobs. All we can do is go by what we know and what we've learned over the years. Sometimes that's not enough.

At the Columbus Zoo, our insurance rates are usually

based on the number of accidents in zoos nationwide. In 1987, we paid $300,000 in liability to cover employees and the public—the figure goes up every year, and it's a huge hunk out of our budget. But knowing as much as I do about the number of things that could go wrong in this business, I consider it money well spent.

/\/\

Since I've been in Columbus, two accidents resulted in serious lawsuits against the zoo—both were settled out of court for considerable sums. I guess in some ways this might be considered an acceptable track record, since we live in an age where if a guy chokes on a Coke from your machine, you'll wind up in court. But I've known all along that the zoo business can be risky business, so I just have to take it as it comes. And when the heat comes down, oh boy do I take it.

During my first year in Columbus, I was involved in a freak accident at a church speech that should never have happened. It was a case of my trying to do too much for too many people. I was very lucky it didn't cost me my job.

I was called to speak at a community church and on short notice present animals before a group of preschool children. Dianna Frisch, who's in charge of apes, had worked with the chimpanzees, and we decided to take two of them along. They are, as everyone knows, very intelligent and entertaining animals. Usually, they can be counted on to make my job easier during a presentation—this is one time they didn't.

We put the male, Cocoa, up on a jungle-gym playground set outside the church to show the kids his climbing ability, with Dianna standing right there next to him. She was pointing out his features and characteristics, and he seemed to be all right, not tensed or stressed in any way. We do this all the time. The kids were, as they always are, very excited, and I was keeping them back. I didn't see one little girl sneak around behind Cocoa.

Before anyone could react, Cocoa grabbed the girl's little

finger, jerked it toward him and bit the end off. It was a terrifying moment that happened lightning fast. With quick thinking, Dianna actually rescued the fingertip from Cocoa's mouth. The girl was rushed to Children's Hospital, and the surgeons reattached the fingertip. We all hoped for the best, but eventually, when the doctors realized the finger wasn't healing properly, it had to be removed altogether.

As we expected, we were sued by the girl's family. After a year or so, they settled out of court. Again, the money is meaningless; how do you price a little girl's finger?

I was sick for that innocent girl, and naturally, a lot of people came down on me. But what I cannot stand in life are the Monday-morning quarterbacks. The same people who had begged me to come to their church were now attacking me. Why did I bring a wild animal? Why did I go to a church where small children were going to school?

I went before the zoo trustees and stressed that I still believed in taking animals out to the public. I said that you have to take systematic chances in life and still try to do what is safe for everybody. Even after all that had happened in my life, I still believed that. They understood and allowed us to continue with certain programs, with limitations, of course—and now, I don't take chimps to schools. I've always been thankful for the trustees' support; taking the zoo out to the people benefits everyone in the long run.

In February 1984, I was in Africa enjoying animals out in the middle of the Serengeti Plain when I received a message that shattered the dream world that I fall into over there. The message came via shortwave radio, garbled in Swahili—translated, it simply said, "Call U.S.A.—there's been an accident at the zoo." That's all.

My heart sank to my stomach. Who? What? Where? I was thousands of miles from home, hundreds of miles from a phone, and all I could find out was that there'd been some sort of mishap at the zoo bad enough so that they had to get in touch with me. They couldn't tell me over the radio what it was that had taken place; they didn't have any details.

I called back over shortwave and asked them to please find out all they could for me, and said that I would radio back in two hours. During that time, I walked around the camp thinking how ironic it was to feel safe surrounded by wild animals while back home something awful had happened with captive animals—I was sure of it.

My worst fears were confirmed when the information finally reached me that a tiger had mauled a woman, that her condition was still undetermined. I wouldn't find out any more than that for two days; it seemed like forever.

The woman was Marikay Cardi, a zoo volunteer in her late twenties whom I had met after speaking to a group of veterinary technicians six months earlier. She seemed nice and sincere when she told me she'd love to work at the zoo. Volunteers provide an important contribution to many zoos; in Columbus, we put people to work based on their desire to help. Marikay Cardi had hardly been there four months

The tiger yard where Marikay Cardi was attacked. (Columbus Zoo file)

when she was attacked by Dolly, a three-hundred-pound Bengal tiger.

As a volunteer, one of Marikay Cardi's jobs was to help clean the tiger exhibit. Of course, this is done while the animal is removed to a separate, caged enclosure.

"All clear" is what the zookeepers yell before releasing an animal back into its habitat. Just prior to the attack, keeper Ernie Tuller called out, checked the enclosure, then came back in and raised the lever on the steel guillotine door that lets the tiger out. That's standard procedure, and Ernie had been doing it for twenty-five years.

Moments later, Ernie heard the terrible screams coming from the yard. He yelled for help and was quickly joined by Dan Hunt, another keeper. They went running into the yard and found the tiger all over Marikay Cardi. Hunt grabbed the only weapon he could find, a broomstick, and began beating the animal off her. The tiger was distracted for a few seconds, long enough to allow them to drag Marikay to safety. She lay there bleeding on the concrete floor as they called for an ambulance.

Marikay Cardi suffered multiple lacerations that required numerous stitches on her arms, legs and head. Fortunately, she survived the accident, and I say fortunately, despite the severe trauma she suffered.

To this day, we don't know exactly how it happened. Ernie told me that he thought that Marikay was already safely back inside, since he didn't see or hear her. Logically, there was only one place she could have been without being seen, and that was behind some rocks, but we can't know that for sure either.

The whole thing might have come out in the negligence suit that was filed against us; however, we chose to settle out of court. It took about three years to settle for a sum somewhere in the neighborhood of a half million dollars.

I always felt terribly bad for Marikay, even after she sued us. But after the lawsuit, we had to totally revamp our program for volunteers. Today, they're not allowed inside any of the animal areas, and I think that's a shame. They can't learn as much about zoo animals and zoo work since they can't work with and watch the keepers anymore. Because of one accident and a major lawsuit, the entire program has suffered.

∧∧

Some animals are a liability no matter how many precautions you take. Koko, our Asian bull elephant, is one of our most prized animals at the Columbus Zoo—he's also one of the most dangerous. At almost five tons, he'd be fearsome with his weight alone, but he's plenty ornery to boot. What he likes to do most is throw things with his trunk.

Koko hates moving objects. We found that out several years ago when he heaved some rocks and knocked out two windshields on the Zephyr, our old tour train. He also smashed my truck windshield the same way when I was driving by his habitat. Koko wears a look on his face like he's always going to get you.

The amazing thing is his accuracy. He's uncanny. Not only can he zing anything he can find, but his delivery is like Nolan Ryan's. He'll pick up a rock and hide it in his trunk, like a pitcher with a ball in his glove, before letting it fly. Naturally, we try to keep his area as missile-free as possible.

Because he's such a menace, we finally decided to let Koko outside only before zoo hours. I was against it at first—being that he's such a magnificent animal, I wanted him out. But the insurance people said they weren't paying for any more train windshields—no more Koko damage, period. So we worked out a system to have him out every morning from six-thirty to ten. Zoo patrons would have to see him behind glass inside the pachyderm house after 10 A.M.

One day a few summers ago, the front gates had opened maybe a few minutes early, or maybe Koko was a little late going back in—one or the other. At any rate, a man and his family managed to go over by the elephant yard while Koko was still out. While the man was walking around innocently, Koko reached up with his trunk and pulled a rock out of one of the decorative planter boxes that are about twelve feet over his head. The elephant fired one of his patented fastballs, and from about forty or fifty feet, he nailed this poor guy right smack in the middle of the forehead.

The victim, Glen Honaker, went right down. No one had any idea what happened—they didn't see it. All that his wife and kids knew was that all of a sudden Dad's on the ground bleeding. I was on the scene almost right away, and I knew it was Koko's work just as soon as I saw that rock lying nearby.

The Honakers were nice, understanding people and they didn't sue. Maybe they saw some humor in the situation. For one thing, the guy'll always have a heck of a story to tell ("I never knew what hit me"). They seemed happy with the zoo passes, posters and what not that I offered them, and, of course, I paid the medical bill, since Mr. Honaker needed some stitches. I wanted them to come back; I thought they might have the wrong idea about our zoo.

That elephant is always a liability. One of our more recent expenses was $76,000 for four outside elephant doors that weigh eight thousand pounds apiece. The old ones just wouldn't hold him. I'm still worried about the two-foot-thick walls—he likes to bang on everything.

One of the neatest things about an elephant is his trunk. That thing has about forty thousand muscles in it, and with it he can do anything from picking up a peanut to moving a thousand-pound log. The day before our Zoofari fund-raiser, Koko lifted up a manhole cover and flipped it like a Frisbee through a $5,000 viewing window. If it had been one day later, it would have taken some heads off. Since then, we've had those covers welded shut. But that's Koko.

The day that Koko beaned a visitor was a bad day. Hardly a half hour after the rock incident, a man broke his arm trying to steal a Coke from a machine up on the Nature Trail. He had his arm halfway up the machine, and the whole thing fell on top of him. Bricker called me on the radio from the accident scene to tell me the guy was going to sue, but I told him to throw the guy out. It wasn't my fault that slob was trying to steal a Coke. That's the difference between people—on one side, you have a gentleman who gets hit by a rock thrown by an elephant and gets up smiling; on the other, some jerk wants to sue you after trying to steal from you.

∧∧

Another frivolous—or at least I'll call it frivolous—threat of a lawsuit occurred just before I got to Columbus. I really should have been here for that one, because it was tailormade for me. Jim McGuire has been the zoo attorney for twenty years, and he told me he was glad this one didn't go to court.

A woman and her kids were walking through the children's zoo when her shoelace came untied. She bent down to tie it and was mounted and humped by a donkey. Her kids all started laughing like crazy, and she was both frightened and humiliated. When she got home, she was still so mad she called the zoo and said she wanted to sue. But when she realized the whole incident would have to be made even more public, she had to drop it—she couldn't take any further embarrassment. I can sympathize, but I'm sorry I missed that one.

On the subject of lawsuits, I'm forever thankful for the attitude of our employees. There are few animals here that don't involve some type of risk in just simple, everyday care. Minor (and sometimes major) injuries are commonplace, and the staff accepts that as part of the job, not as an excuse to go running for a lawyer.

Now, I'm not saying that if Koko kills a keeper—and he's capable—we won't be sued. That elephant has banged a lot of my people around. Don Winstel, who's now our curator, was thrown against a wall ten feet in the air during one of Koko's fits. During that same brouhaha, Brad Booth had his head gashed. But what I like about these guys is that they can pretty much laugh these things off later—they know the risks come with the job.

Dan Badgley, our head reptile keeper, had a very serious

accident after being here eighteen years. A spitting cobra got him in the eyes. It takes just one second, one mistake. He took the top off a bucket and the snake let him have it. He was smart; he didn't panic. He lay back while his co-workers flushed water into his eyes. It burned like crazy, but his eyesight was saved. He's still got some spots in his eyes from the damage.

Once, one of our red pandas got out during a snowstorm. These are small, cute animals, weighing at most maybe ten to twelve pounds. This one didn't go far and crawled up

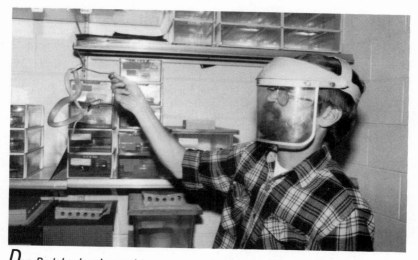

*D*an Badgley has learned to wear a mask when handling spitting cobras. (Columbus Zoo, Nancy Staley)

into a snowbank. Ernie Tuller netted it, then tried to grab it with his free hand. With its knife-sharp teeth, that thing about tore his thumb off, ripped his whole hand up. Any animal will bite. *Any* animal.

A zoo director can't always be aware of everything going on in all of the zoo's various departments. You try to know as much as possible about your animals, but you delegate authority. If you've got really good people working for you, it's easy to lose touch with some day-to-day operations. I found this out one day in the form of one outrageous insurance claim.

Don Winstel has been at the zoo since he was fourteen years old. When I got to Columbus, he had worked himself up to being in charge of the pachyderm collection. He's a quiet, soft-spoken guy, and I always thought those guys over in pachyderms were a neat group and very dedicated to their job. Mostly, it's because they work with these massive mammals—hippos, rhinos, elephants, tapirs—and also because they have the thankless task of removing huge quantities of crap all day. It's a never-ending process. What goes in must come out, right?

Anyway, I pretty much left those guys alone when I first got here. The animals were in great shape, so they obviously knew what they were doing.

At that time, I was saddled with a great deal of paperwork, and I often wound up signing checks late into the night. One day, I noticed an insurance form on my desk along with a claim for a lost contact lens from Don Winstel. The claim said that the lens had been knocked out of his eye while he was masturbating a black rhinoceros to collect semen. What? So I'm supposed to ask the insurance company for sixty-five dollars for a lens that was lost while ejaculating a rhino? No way! There was no way in hell I was going to sign that claim.

It was the first I'd heard about this anyway, so I ran up to the pachyderm building to see what was going on. The guys told me they'd been masturbating Clyde, our black rhino, once a week for about three or four months. They would drive his sperm down to the Cincinnati Zoo, where it could be frozen and preserved for artificial insemination.

Their method was archaic, but quite ingenious. At the front end, someone would feed Clyde monkey chow. (To my knowledge, Clyde is the only rhino in the world who'll eat monkey chow—which is like a sweet biscuit—and at the same time stand still for this type of research.) At the other end, they had this contraption made from two two-by-fours that held a soft rubber femur cast (used for broken

*K*eeper Andy Lodge feeding Clyde the rhino monkey chow, which gets him excited.
(Columbus Zoo, Rick Prebeg)

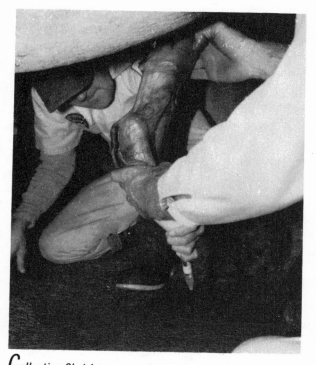

*C*ollecting Clyde's semen, which is frozen for later use in artificial insemination, may
be the black rhino's last chance for survival. (Columbus Zoo, Nancy Staley)

legs). They would slide this thing back and forth until Clyde ejaculated and the semen collected in one end of the cast. Every Monday morning, they'd gather about six ounces of the stuff that way. Of course, Clyde was having a great time. He probably lit up when he saw the keepers approaching him.

Artificial insemination may be one of the black rhino's last chances for survival. No artificial inseminations have yet been successful anywhere, but when they are, Clyde may provide for future offspring—with the help of the crew up at pachyderms (who since have developed more sophisticated collection techniques). But there was no way I could file that insurance claim. I reimbursed Don for his contact lens out of petty cash.

⋀⋀

We must never forget that most zoo animals are wild animals with all of the defensive and aggressive instincts of their free-ranging cousins. The public often misunderstands this when they see keepers interacting with the animals. Giving the gorilla a drink from a glass through the mesh. Scratching a zebra's ears while the other hand rubs its back. Mowing the cheetah yard as the cats roam freely. Rubbing a great cat's nose through the bars. Romping with the baby orangutans in the nursery. Entering the eagle cage to clean. Handling young exotics and native wildlife on outreaches or television. Training and handling the elephants.

What the envious visitor often does not understand (despite our educational efforts) is that the keeper may have raised that animal from birth, may have years of relationship with the animal and most .certainly is trained in animal handling and behavior. Keepers know the behavior of the species and also, in most cases, the behavior of the individual animal. They know which is predictable, which is unpredictable. Some animals seem to enjoy and solicit interaction. Others are never touched under any circumstances.

Even the most tractable, usually reliable animal may behave defensively or aggressively under out-of-the-ordinary conditions. The bull elephant in musth gives no second chances. The bull moose in rut (breeding season) is not the same creature that browses in his yard at other times of the year. Mothers (and sometimes fathers, too) with young may be instinctively willing to protect their offspring to the death. And then there are the individual idiosyncrasies: at Columbus, some of our primates engage in sexual discrimination, with the gibbons disliking men and the capuchin monkeys disliking women. And, of course, legends abound from zoo to zoo about the gorillas, chimps and orangs and their thoughtfully worked-out escape attempts—everything from picking locks with bits of salvaged wire to propping logs against moat walls to make the big break.

Some animals, especially those normally preyed upon in the wild, such as some hoofed stock, are especially shy or easily frightened into running. A routine of calm handling and quiet conditions help to avoid possible injury to either keeper or animals.

Anything with teeth can bite. Anything with claws can scratch. Anything with horns can gore. Anything with talons can tear. And anything that is wild is wild. And our keepers and handlers never forget this. A keeper is usually allowed one mistake if he or she is lucky, because, I'm sorry to say, any mistake may be fatal. A wild animal is like a loaded gun, capable of going off at any time. Behind the scenes, each department has its own set of transfer, cleaning, feeding and safety procedures that must be followed by everyone working there. One person's carelessness may cause a fellow employee and/or an animal to be injured. They must be responsible for each other.

On the outside, our fences, barriers and warning signs aren't there just so we can impose meaningless authority. The visitors who don't obey these restrictions, placed there for their own safety, may be injured or at the very least asked to leave the park if they can't heed the warnings. We want each visitor's stay to be pleasant, and safe, and we must and do take precautions very seriously.

*C*olo, the first lowland gorilla born in captivity, three months old.
(*Columbus Citizen Journal*)

10

GORILLAS
IN
OUR
MIDST

*M*any people, and some zoo directors, will argue that gorillas are the most fascinating and intriguing of all zoo animals. They've got a good argument, but I don't want to make that statement, only because I have too much respect for all the animals. I say the same thing when people ask me what my favorite animal is—hey, it may sound corny, but I love 'em all.

But the gorillas here in Columbus have always been a special attraction. It all dates back to Mac and Millie, two wild-caught gorillas who were brought to the Columbus Zoo in 1951. Mac and Millie obviously hit it off, and the result was Colo, the first gorilla born in captivity. That day, December 22, 1956, made zoo history.

Colo herself would go on to have three offspring—Emmy, Oscar and Toni, all prize winners—and they, with some outside help from breeding loans, would continue to build our family tree. By 1988, there had been twenty gorilla births in Columbus, a phenomenal number when you consider how difficult captive gorilla breeding is. Maybe it's something in the water here. I keep saying they ought to bring us those pandas who have so much trouble mating. They'd reproduce here, for sure.

Our collection is the second or third largest in the United

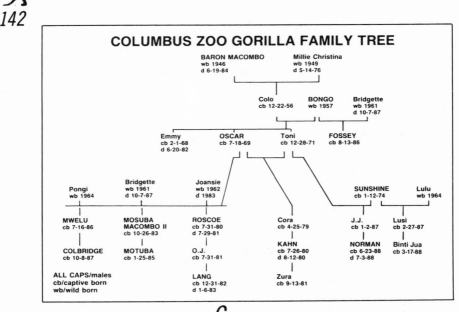

COLUMBUS ZOO GORILLA FAMILY TREE

BARON MACOMBO
wb 1946
d 6-19-84

Millie Christina
wb 1949
d 5-14-76

Colo
cb 12-22-56

BONGO
wb 1957

Bridgette
wb 1961
d 10-7-87

Emmy
cb 2-1-68
d 6-20-82

OSCAR
cb 7-18-69

Toni
cb 12-28-71

FOSSEY
cb 8-13-86

Pongi
wb 1964

Bridgette
wb 1961
d 10-7-87

Joansie
wb 1962
d 1983

SUNSHINE
cb 1-12-74

Lulu
wb 1964

MWELU
cb 7-16-86

MOSUBA
MACOMBO II
cb 10-26-83

ROSCOE
cb 7-31-80
d 7-29-81

Cora
cb 4-25-79

J.J.
cb 1-2-87

Lusi
cb 2-27-87

COLBRIDGE
cb 10-8-87

MOTUBA
cb 1-25-85

O.J.
cb 7-31-81

KAHN
cb 7-26-80
d 8-12-80

NORMAN
cb 6-23-88
d 7-3-88

Binti Jua
cb 3-17-88

ALL CAPS/males
cb/captive born
wb/wild born

LANG
cb 12-31-82
d 1-6-83

Zura
cb 9-13-81

*G*orilla family tree. (Family Tree: Julie Estadt)

States. Thirty-one-year-old Bongo is the oldest reproducing male in captivity, and Oscar, with his eleven offspring, is one of the most prolific male gorillas in captivity. With every new birth, I feel like a proud father. Yes, I do pass out cigars.

Breeding animals in captivity is one of the main purposes of zoos today. This goes a long way toward the survival of many species. We don't want to put animals in a sterile environment and let people gawk at them—that was the old zoo. Today we're trying to pair animals up in environments conducive to breeding. Of course, we can't give them a choice of fifty different mates. You just do the best that you can do and hope the animals get along.

At our zoo, what we try to do is to fulfill their basic needs and ensure their comfort so that their natural behavior can operate within a family structure, the same as it would in the wild—with the males leading and protecting and the females being submissive. Then breeding can occur.

With the captive "selection" process, you never know, so you just have to take each case individually. One pair may prefer seclusion for breeding and need to be pulled from their group. Or a frightened female may suppress ovulation; in this case, she may have to be removed and later reintroduced to the male. The males are up to two times larger than their mates and can get rough, so it's a potentially scary and stressful experience, especially for a first-time female.

We also look for certain signs. With gorillas, play behavior is very similar to breeding behavior, as far as vocalizations and positioning are concerned. If the female trusts the male enough to allow him to scratch her or tickle her from behind, that's good. The same with nuzzling on the shoulder. Then the chances of breeding are very good. You never really know, but in Columbus we've been lucky most of the time.

∧∧

Most of the captive gorillas worldwide are western lowland gorillas, rather than mountain gorillas, like those seen in *Gorillas in the Mist*, the film about the late primatologist Dian Fossey. There are few behavioral differences between the two subspecies; physically, the mountain gorillas are stockier-looking with more and longer hair.

Western lowland gorillas are found in equatorial West Africa and number somewhere around 10,000 animals. The extremely endangered mountain gorillas live solely in the Virunga Mountains of central Africa (Rwanda, Zaire and Uganda). In 1981, the Rwandan population declined to about 254 gorillas, and it was feared that this subspecies, which wasn't discovered until the twentieth century, might not survive the same century. Today, due largely to antipoaching efforts, their numbers have risen to 293 in 1988. A few more, perhaps a hundred, exist outside the census area. However, as long as loss of habitat (mostly due to farming) remains a serious threat, their future will remain uncertain. To the east live a few hundred members of a

A rare mountain gorilla, photographed in Rwanda. There are probably no more than 400 left in existence. (Rick Prebeg)

third subspecies, the eastern lowland gorilla. All gorillas are endangered.

Several organizations work on behalf of the mountain gorilla. The one with whom we have been most closely associated is the Digit Fund, established by Dian Fossey in honor of her favorite gorilla, Digit, who was slaughtered by poachers. The fund supports the Karisoke Research Centre, which she founded in Rwanda, and has been administered by the Morris Animal Foundation since Dian's murder in 1985. We've done some fund-raising on their behalf and attempt to publicize their efforts whenever possible.

In 1988, we gave ourselves a special gift—our own mountain gorilla. The gorilla was adopted through a program initiated by the Digit Fund. Little Intwlai, born in 1986, will stay with her wild parents, Puck and Ziz, in the mountains of Rwanda—we will follow her life with great interest and can only hope that she gets the chance to grow into a very old lady with many descendants who will roam those mountains forever.

∧∧∧

Before Columbus, I'd seen very few gorillas, and all were caged. Putting the gorillas outside when I first got here just seemed like a natural to me. The Atlanta Zoo made great strides for all captive apes when they recently built Willie B., their star male gorilla, and his friends a big $3.5 million outdoor yard. It's a phenomenal enclosure, one of the finest ever built, but I'm still proud of the fact that we originally put our guys outside for $50,000.

Actually, we stole a page out of Willie B.'s book when we got a color TV for Mac back in 1979. At that time, it was national news how Willie B. was a big pro football fan and had his own TV set. Sandy Holton, a local television dealer, read about this and called to ask me if any of our gorillas were lonely and would like a free color set. Mac had lost his mate three years earlier, so I said sure, I thought it was a great idea. Well, Mac wasn't all that nuts about the set, but he did go bananas for the warranty, which somebody had left lying around. He ate that in a couple of bites, then went to work on the *TV Guide* I bought him. The keepers swore he liked game shows and sports, and was particularly fascinated by *The Planet of the Apes*!

Largely because they have such human characteristics, and also partly because they almost always get named, gorillas hold a special place in zoos. In 1979, we had a contest to name a female baby, the first third-generation gorilla born in captivity. The contest drew over two thousand entries, with Cora chosen as the winning name—I'm not sure exactly how. But communities become very attached to their gorilla population, if their zoo is fortunate enough to have one. I found this out when Emmy died up in Cleveland while there on a breeding loan. People around here were very upset.

Massa, the gorilla who passed away a few years ago in Philadelphia, was an institution. He lived to be fifty-four, the oldest captive gorilla in the world—and he represented the first and oldest zoo in the country. When he died, a part of the city of Philadelphia died with him.

Every time we have a gorilla birth, it's a major event. Our local media (and sometimes national) await the birth and treat it just like they would any celebrity's. It's more tradition than it is my going out and hyping it. Then after the birth, on a weekend, thousands of people visit the zoo to see the new gorilla mother with her baby. It's a zoo phenomenon, always fascinating to watch.

Also, it's inevitable that you have visitors with the King Kong thing. They'll be crowding around the habitat, beating their chests and scratching their armpits, and saying stuff like "That big sucker can break that glass anytime he wants. I'll be the first one out of the building!" Sometimes I think they really would like to see one get out—at a safe distance, of course. That's no different from wanting to see race cars crash. If it sells, I guess I shouldn't complain, but gorillas aren't that way, and we try to tell people that. They're really gentle giants.

Many of our visitors are becoming increasingly respectful and knowledgeable about our gorillas, recognizing them by sight, asking for them by name and following their fortunes and misfortunes like they do soap operas. This is very much due to the educational efforts of staff and volunteers and also, beginning in 1986, due to seeing babies being raised by their moms and dads.

The unique combination of gentleness and power is what makes gorilla watching so fascinating to me, whether it's in the wilds of Africa or at the Columbus Zoo. Having a four-hundred-pound lowland gorilla come up to within two feet of you and look directly into your eyes is mind-blowing.

*C*olo, like all gorillas at the time, lived behind bars. Our outdoor habitat was built in 1980. Now most captive gorillas live in natural habitats. (Columbus Citizen Journal)

You're trying to figure out what he's thinking; at the same time, that's probably what he's trying to do with you.

I've watched a gorilla take a master padlock that I wouldn't be able to dent with pliers and a blowtorch, take that thing and squash it like a marshmallow. I've seen a gorilla take a green-shelled coconut and pop it open like a peanut. At the same time, you have the wonder of a Bongo, our 420-pound, thirty-two-year-old patriarch, raising Fossey, his son, after the mother, Bridgette, died when the baby was just a little over a year old. When Fossey was maybe fifteen pounds, Bongo would play with him the same way a human being might handle delicate crystalware.

A good example of the combination of strength and

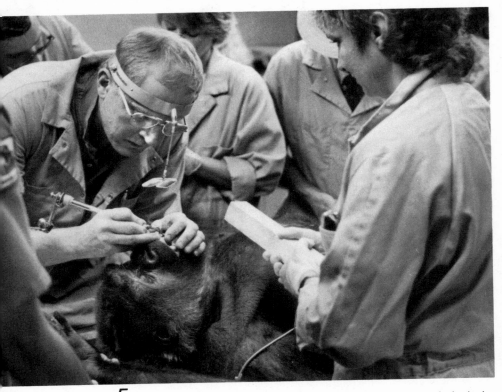

*E*ven gorillas go to the dentist. Our gorillas get complete annual physicals.
(Columbus Citizen Journal, Arlen Pennell)

gentleness that gorillas have occurred in my first year here. It was a stunt involving superhuman strength that I allowed to happen, but probably wouldn't get involved with today because of all the flak I'd take from fellow zoo directors.

Just after we had moved the gorillas outdoors, a man from a consumer-protective cable network in the Midwest called to ask if we would allow some sort of test involving luggage and an ape. What they wanted to do was put a Samsonite suitcase in with a gorilla to see what would happen.

I was curious myself, so I said all right, provided the gorilla can't get hurt by the suitcase and provided he's by himself. The consumer agency was looking to disprove the claim about the supposed strength of the luggage that was appearing on a national commercial at the time. And that's just what they did, with Bongo's help.

We chose Bongo, since he's fairly interactive with objects, and we had the suitcase handle taken off so he wouldn't hurt himself. When we first put the suitcase in, Bongo examined it and sniffed it the way gorillas check out any new object—he had obviously never seen a suitcase before. He fiddled with it for a few minutes, and then, amazingly, he popped it open at the latches with his thumbs, just the way anyone else would do it. He opened it up, laid it out and looked at it real quietly for a couple of minutes. Then he lifted it with both hands, brought it up in front of him, and opened it backwards, bending it back like he was playing the accordion. That suitcase was now completely mangled and totally unusable. He finished it off by hurling it against a wall, breaking it in two.

I see nothing wrong with having the public fantasize or compare human strength or size with gorillas. We make molds of gorillas' hands and then let people put their hands up next to them to compare. It's fun and educational.

Once, during a gorilla's physical exam—they get yearly physicals, just like people—I had the keepers measure Bongo's waistline. Of course, this was done when he was anesthetized—a gorilla would no more let you put your hands around his waist than he would let you pick his nose. We had some pants made up, and now, when I'm speaking to children, I'll have three or four kids come up and fit into Bongo's trousers. We do the same thing with shirts (size 22 necks). It's one way of letting people know how big the gorilla is and what a magnificent animal he is.

All zoo animals have controlled diets, and a good indicator of how healthy the animals are is how well they breed. Our gorillas eat a quality of produce that is probably equal to what you might find in New York City's finest restaurants, maybe better.

A typical day's feed for Bongo would begin with a breakfast of grapefruit, apple, sometimes a boiled egg, lettuce or spinach, cooked sweet potatoes, a banana, carrots and vitamins. For lunch, there would be a snack consisting of yogurt and a special protein drink developed by the Ape House staff. During the day, they're kept busy with sunflower seeds, which they shell with their teeth, monkey biscuits and willow branches to forage on. Sometimes they have a special treat of sugarcane, coconut or watermelon. For dinner, they get bok choy and endive, more sweet potatoes and carrots, onions, fruit and a white potato.

Pregnant females and sick gorillas also get broiled liver, while those with colds get hot onion/garlic soup run through a blender and served in a glass. They do all right.

Despite the four-star diet, and all the care we can provide, there will always be problems. One of the most trying experiences in my zoo career was a year-long struggle to keep a baby gorilla named Roscoe alive.

Oscar, Roscoe's father, is such a great lover that we had a hard time keeping tabs on his offspring. At least that was the case when one of his mates, Joansie, a nineteen-year-old gorilla on loan from the Buffalo Zoo, gave a surprise premature birth to a male in July 1980. We weren't sure she was pregnant, and we thought she might be overweight. Besides, Oscar seemed to ignore her; his real favorite among his females was Toni, a nine-year-old who had given birth to a male earlier the same week.

Both new babies had to be "pulled" from their mothers because of inadequate maternal care. We usually leave a baby with its mother up to forty-eight hours. If by that time the mother hasn't begun to nurse the baby, it has to be taken to the animal nursery, where it can be nurtured and bottle-fed. This is standard procedure in zoos, and it sometimes happens with captive gorilla mothers since they often don't know how to nurse. In the wild, they learn within the family, as with everything else. Until fairly recently in captivity, they haven't had that opportunity.

Some people think we raise gorillas in the nursery so that the public can walk up to the window and go, "Oh, isn't he cute. Look at that little gorilla in his diaper getting a bottle."

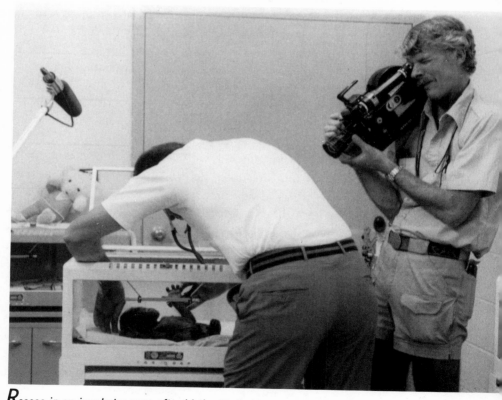

*R*oscoe in an incubator soon after birth. (Columbus Zoo, Rick Prebeg)

That's not it at all. We don't like to pull babies because natural motherhood is best, and also because it's prohibitively expensive, costing up to $35,000 a year just in nursery salaries alone.

After two weeks in the nursery, Toni's baby died quite suddenly of a bacterial infection that we couldn't catch in time. We knew Joansie's baby was in trouble as well, probably with the same thing. I don't like to name zoo babies until they make it to two or three months, because I'd rather have to announce, "The gorilla baby died today," than I would, "Billy Joe died." Roscoe, Joansie's baby, lasted a year, so he was named for Ross Hall at Children's Hospital, where he spent most of his life.

The entire ordeal with Roscoe was a heartrending, uphill-downhill struggle. At first, we tried to keep him on formula, but his condition worsened and he wouldn't gain weight. He seemed to be suffering the same illness that took his half brother's life—something we unfortunately knew little about. One morning, three days after the first baby died, Roscoe was going down the tubes pretty fast, and we decided to rush him to the animal research wing at Children's Hospital.

Roscoe was afflicted with a bacterial infection in his stomach and intestines. Before he was five weeks old, he had to go on a life-support system. Over the first months of his short life, his condition improved enough a few times so that he could be brought back to his nonsterile environment at the zoo, but he would always deteriorate and have to return to the hospital.

Everyone involved—doctors, veterinarians and zoo staff—soon realized that Roscoe couldn't live without the life support. It was an expensive proposition, due to reach over $2,000 a month in medical costs alone, to keep him alive—this was with all personnel donating their time. Our yearly medical budget at the zoo totaled only about $18,000 at the time, so if we wanted to keep Roscoe around, we'd have to find more money, which we did,

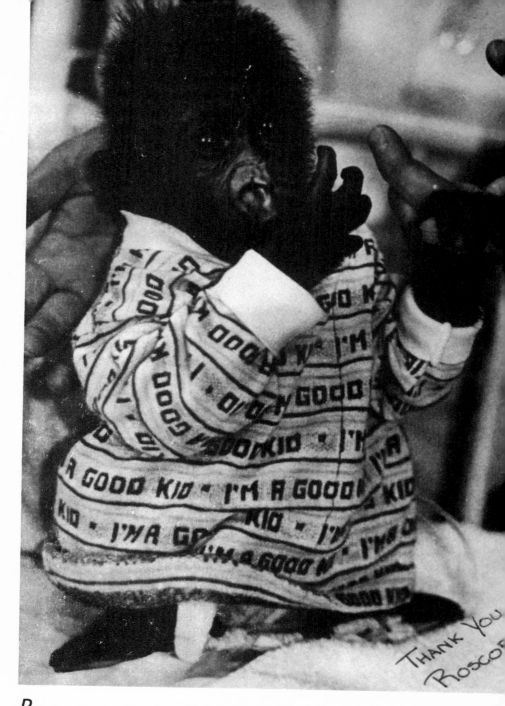

THANK YOU
ROSCOE

Roscoe, who lived for a year on a life-support system, won the hearts of all Ohio. (United Press International, Sue Ogrocki)

mostly through fund-raising and donations. It was a tough, controversial decision.

In my mind, there was never really any choice about what to do. Aside from the basic "keep living things alive at all cost" philosophy that I have, there were other factors: (1) gorillas are endangered, vanishing fast, and must be protected—as best as possible, (2) gorillas are economically quite valuable and worth as much as $150,000 apiece and (3) primate research has been invaluable in saving human lives—here was our chance to repay the debt.

The ordeal also touched me personally, because of my daughter's struggle at the very same hospital. Julie, my youngest, was fighting leukemia at the very same time. Her disease was in remission, but she still had to undergo bone-marrow tests and spinal injections. Every night when I got home, Julie would ask me, "How's the baby gorilla?" I thought to myself, my daughter's alive because of research that's been done on animals.

The arguments over such research, especially on primates, will probably rage for a long time to come. This is a moral issue that pits animal rights advocates against those supporting research that benefits human life in varying degrees. There are serious and legitimate questions to be dealt with on both sides, and we certainly can't answer them here. I do know that Julie benefited from the research, and for that my family and I will be forever grateful.

So thanks to community support, we kept Roscoe going. Throughout all of his rallies and setbacks, the people of central Ohio were wonderful: the doctors—like Richard McLead, who was with him from day one—and nurses who donated their time, not just treating Roscoe but training zoo staff to aid in noncritical care; the zoo staff, people like Marsha King and Chris Pendleton, who spent long shifts and sleepless nights caring for the little guy; working people who donated money to defray costs; schoolchildren who helped with the fund-raising—all these and many more not only kept Roscoe going but kept a positive spirit alive around the zoo.

After just two days short of one year of intravenous feedings and intermittent life support, Roscoe's life mercifully ended. He died of congestive heart failure in Chris's arms. Chris, who'd probably spent more time than anyone with him, told me often that he had such a personality, she'd always consider him her friend. She wasn't alone. Dr. McLead was too upset to do the autopsy.

With his courageous struggle to stay alive, Roscoe touched many hearts, but his hospital stay was not in vain. We learned a great deal about gorilla infancy and dehydration that would go a long way toward saving similarly afflicted animals in the future. It had only been two years since we'd given the gorillas their new back yard, but I realized now, more than ever, how important these animals were to our zoo and the animal world.

But Roscoe's story didn't end on a totally sad note. Two days after he died, on his first birthday, Joansie, his mother, gave birth to another male, also fathered by Oscar. This tyke survived just fine, but we eventually sent him to the Buffalo Zoo to honor a prior breeding-loan arrangement.

Gorillas live in family groups, each led by a dominant mature male and each containing one or more females and their infants. Generally, the groups are kept separate. When I first arrived in Columbus, we had two groups. Today, we have four, led by Bongo, Oscar, Mumbah and Sunshine. As our gorilla population at the zoo expanded in the early 1980s, we realized we had to continue to upgrade and expand their habitat.

Some of the pain of Roscoe's death was overcome in 1983 by the birth of twin sons to Bridgette and Oscar. The story of this exciting and unusual event is told elsewhere, in the chapter on zoo births. These two bright-eyed, "smiling" little guys put the gorilla program on the map once again and ultimately brought about the beginnings of our relationship with *Good Morning America*.

But births mean more animals and more animals mean more and better space. In 1984, thanks to a capital improvement fund, we spent $650,000 to remodel the interior of

Bongo plays with his son, Fossey. (Columbus Zoo, Nancy Staley)

the old Ape House and to build a new outdoor habitat complete with jungle canopy for our gorilla families. The 9,000-square-foot wire mesh and metal enclosure was modeled after a similar, smaller structure that a group of us from the zoo had seen in England a year earlier.

We'd been visiting the private zoo of John Aspinall, a maverick animal lover in Canterbury, England, who has a spectacular collection of apes. Aspinall was an unconventional guy—he'd give his gorillas a cold beer now and then, and he'd even go in and physically play with them, sometimes getting himself seriously hurt. But we were knocked out by his "Gorilla Villa," and decided after returning home that that would be just the ticket for our guys.

The enclosure took six months to build and opened in May in front of television cameras, a small crowd looking on through large viewing windows and an anxious zoo staff. As with the staff-remodeled facility built five years earlier, the yard took some getting used to by our captive-bred primates. In addition to the wire mesh that was supposed to serve for climbing, we had yards of ropes and swings built in, which none of them seemed to go for. Too many years on cement floors, I guess. I crawled around in there myself before it was opened and had a lot of fun, but that's me.

The problem was that, for the gorillas, a rope didn't mean something to swing on; it didn't mean anything, since they'd never seen a jungle vine. Many of them, due to age and habit, didn't particularly feel like climbing either, and I took a lot of ribbing while they just sat happily on the ground. We had some volunteers try swinging around in front of the apes, but that just about put them to sleep.

Later that summer, we received a new male, nineteen-year-old Mumbah, on loan from John Aspinall. Mumbah was coming over to try to breed with Toni and start a new family, but the media made a big thing about how Mumbah would come over and "show our gorillas the ropes." I thought it was possible, since he'd been raised with Aspinall's gorillas, who had had ropes for years. But Mumbah got

Mumbah helped our gorillas learn the ropes. (Columbus Zoo, Nancy Staley)

in there and never swung on those ropes, although he does use the swag ropes as a hammock for afternoon siestas.

It's a popular theory that gorillas learn by imitation, by copying, but it doesn't always work out that way. I guess we're probably too often influenced by the verb "ape," meaning to imitate, to mimic. One of my brilliant ideas back in 1980 only served to show me that if a gorilla ain't interested, you can forget about it, whatever it is you're trying to show him, or her, as the case was.

Dian Fossey had proven with her studies in Africa that the gorilla is a very social animal and, like human beings, can learn by watching others. In the late 1970s the theory was so popular it was said that some zoos were screening sexually explicit films for apes who had difficulty breeding. I don't know if that worked or not, but I can say that Oscar never had any problems in that respect. He knows exactly how it's done.

Anyway, I was getting very frustrated watching baby gorillas being pulled from their mothers who couldn't nurse. It was a Catch-22 situation—we couldn't leave such valuable and endangered infant animals at risk, yet how was the mother gorilla ever supposed to learn?

So one day I looked into the possibility of having a woman nurse a baby—live, not on film—in front of the gorillas. Maybe then they'd learn how to do it. I knew it sounded wacky, but I didn't think I'd have any trouble getting volunteers. When Roscoe was sick, we got a lot of calls from ladies asking if we needed their milk.

I called La Leche League, the breast-feeding organization, and they said they'd love to help out. I assured them there'd be complete privacy, except for a few zoo staff members. They sent over a young mother who was very nice and, most important, enthusiastic. This wasn't any everyday thing—Mel Dodge had already told me I was nuts on this one.

Of course, we had a window separating the lady from the gorillas, and I told her she should get as close as possible. Well, as with Mumbah and the ropes, those females, Toni and Joansie, weren't interested. They looked up, the same as when visitors come in, but they didn't really pay attention.

Oscar was another story. He moved in for a ringside seat. He was definitely fascinated—had his nose flush against the glass, but it wasn't as if he had to shove anybody out of the way. So the whole thing kind of fizzled out. Again, we got some national attention on this one, with the newspapers, Paul Harvey's radio show and what not. I still think it's a good idea; maybe I'll try it again someday in front of some different female gorillas.

Since most of the gorillas aren't crazy about me—I'll

explain this momentarily—I can easily say that Oscar is my favorite. Oscar is a character. He knows me—I call him "Oscar Mayer Wiener." If I've had a hard day, I might wait until the zoo's empty, take a walk and go sit down in the bleachers we have opposite the gorillas. I'll call out, "Hey, Wiener, how ya doin'?" He'll look over at me, and if I've got some grapes, he'll come over. I'll feed him the grapes and he'll grunt, which is a friendly-type thing.

I think Oscar and I have an understanding. Since I don't have a lot of time to spend with most of the animals at the zoo, they don't recognize me, and I don't expect them to. But Oscar is one who does recognize me, and I appreciate it when he does. He's my buddy. He's a guy I can talk to . . . and he doesn't talk back. His day has always been

Oscar, my favorite gorilla. On top of being a character, Oscar is also quite a stud.
(Columbus Zoo, Nancy Staley)

*J*ungle Jack and his namesake, JJ. (Columbus Zoo, Nancy Staley)

pretty good—he eats plenty and he mates whenever he wants. He's a family man.

I don't take it personally, but gorillas respond to body language. Sometimes I move too fast or talk too loud, and they can't really deal with that. They're primates, which comes from the word "primary," and they're very basic in everything they do.

Another thing: male humans are often threatening to gorillas, especially to male gorillas. They often feel threatened by beards, which fortunately I don't have. But they respond better to women. I really have to watch myself when I come in the Ape House—I have to cool my heels, and sometimes I forget. Once, right after Christmas, I went in there wearing a brand-new suede coat that I'd received as a present. I wasn't in there two minutes before Bongo had thrown shit all over it, ruined it. At close range, they're very accurate—they'll throw right between the bars. It's one of their favorite defenses. They'll pick out a person they don't like, and they'll splatter him.

The Ape House staff does a tremendous job with our great-ape collection. The staff is made up of all women, which some people tell me is sort of reverse sexism, but I don't see it that way.

First of all, the success of our great apes speaks for itself. Somebody has to be doing something right, and Dianna and her staff proved themselves in this regard a long time ago. Second, there's no way a man can go in there and out-macho a gorilla. You've got to out-think them. Women's movements are smoother, they're quieter, and the gorillas prefer that.

Now, I'm not saying men can't be ape keepers; there are many excellent ones in this country. But I've never seen Bongo throw anything at a woman, ever. Our keepers give the gorillas drinks from a glass, put food in their mouths and tickle their bellies. I'd get killed trying to do that.

Once a year, we have a practice session for a dangerous-animal escape. Only I and two other people will know in advance, and it involves getting the police, a SWAT team helicopter and the zoo staff coordinated in case anything ever happened. We usually practice on a crowded day in springtime; otherwise we wouldn't learn anything. Of course, the public gets upset, since we have to evacuate the zoo.

One late August day in 1982, I was talking to someone about rhino insemination when the call came over the radio that a gorilla was loose. My first thought was, there's no practice today, and then it hit me that this was the real thing. I tried to find out more, but everybody was screaming all at once. I flew out of my office and went running across the zoo grounds to the Ape House. Once I got there, I saw security people already beginning evacuation. I thought, oh my God.

Bricker was there, and he had his gun ready. In our business there's a rule, and that is that if a human being is in danger, then there's really no decision—the animal has to be shot. With zoo rules, human life takes precedence— no matter what. If you can tranquilize the animal, that's fine, but a lot of times tranquilization takes quite a while. The animal may not be trying to hurt anyone, but he's in an atmosphere he's not familiar with and can be dangerous.

So Bricker, the curators and the keepers were all there within minutes, people were on their way out and I remember thinking, thank goodness for our practice sessions.

Meanwhile, Oscar was loose in the Ape House—not running around the grounds or anything, just loose in the keeper aisles outside his cage. A mistake had been made, a cage door had been left unlocked. It sounds crazy, I know, that a cage door gets left open, but with what I know about human error, I'm surprised it doesn't happen more often.

The keeper aisle is behind the enclosures; there are phones, sinks, hoses, all kinds of stuff back there. There's also one door separating that area from the outside world— one door with one little doorknob. All Oscar had to do was turn that doorknob.

Oscar was having a ball in there—we could hear that much. He was tearing spigots off sinks, pulling pipes off the wall, ripping up rubber hoses, preoccupied with everything. He'd been watching the keepers for years; this was his shot to do anything he wanted.

I wasn't sure what to do about the door—it was only a matter of minutes until he got bored with what he was doing, and I knew we couldn't hold that door. There was a worker nearby with a backhoe, and it occurred to me to commandeer that thing and push it up against the door. Ten, fifteen seconds after we blocked the door with the backhoe, we saw the doorknob start to turn. We all stared at it like it was something out of an Alfred Hitchcock movie. When Oscar realized something was jammed up against the door, he pounded and pushed, trying to get out. He couldn't, so he went back to making his mess in there.

By this time, Dr. Gardner, our veterinarian, had arrived with a blowgun and tranquilizers. We like to use a blowgun rather than a rifle because it's like a bee sting and there's no noise to scare the animal. Dr. Gardner went up into a loft area above Oscar, shot the dart into Oscar's shoulder and watched him get sleepy. We moved in, locked him up, and only then did I call the newspapers. Oscar has not been out since then.

But I really don't think Oscar would have done anything to anybody. Just a few years ago, there was a report of a little boy who fell into a moat in a gorilla exhibit in England. A big male gorilla went over and touched the boy, who was unconscious, looked at him, and when the child roused and cried, he backed off. That's more the way Oscar is. I was more worried that he might somehow hurt himself on a utility wire or a hot wire in there. But Oscar blew his big chance at a breakout, and I'm glad.

January 2, 1987, was my fortieth birthday, a real downer for some people, but I received one of the best presents I ever got. At about three-thirty that afternoon, I got a call that Toni, the daughter of Bongo and Colo, had just given birth to a male baby. The father was Sunshine, who was on loan to us from the San Francisco Zoo. A baby gorilla on my birthday!

The keepers decided that the zoo wasn't ready for two Jungle Jacks, so they named the baby JJ, in my honor. His mother wasn't able to raise him, so he was reared for fourteen months in the nursery and then turned over to his grandmother, Colo, who took over as his surrogate mother. I don't know what was more satisfying—seeing Colo with that baby or seeing that nursery-raised baby being "all gorilla" in a large family group. I do know that, wherever I go, it will always be satisfying to know that a little part of me is a part of that special family of apes.

Sheba and Skylar, monkey's best friend ... (*Columbus Dispatch*, Tom Dodge)

11

MONKEY BUSINESS— PROMOTING THE ZOO

When I was hired as director of the Columbus Zoo, the job was primarily to sell the zoo to the people of central Ohio. They didn't need a zoological expert, a Ph.D., somebody who knows all the Latin names for animals—which I don't. In fact, I only know a few of them. What I do know is how to promote a zoo.

Since I've been in Columbus, zoo attendance has gone from 350,000 to almost a million visitors a year. The annual budget shot from $1.7 million in 1978 to almost $7 million in 1988. In 1985, a five-year $2.2 million county tax levy for the zoo received a 70 percent favorable vote. To my critics in the zoo world, I can only ask, does anyone think these things would have happened without promoting the place? Would a zoo animal in Columbus be better off if I learned his Latin name, or would it be better off if I went out and raised the money to build the animal a new home?

Most zoos must promote to stay in business. They couldn't survive otherwise. Only a few zoos are self-sustaining. State, county and city funds help, but you need solid, consistent attendance and corporate donations to pull through; the only way to get these is to make people aware of the zoo, make them feel as though they're contributing to a necessary part of the community, a part of the community that's just as important as the symphony, libraries or even the school system.

Like many zoos, the Columbus Zoo is operated by a zoological association. This is a nonprofit corporation composed of a varying number of trustees and an executive board that is appointed to operate the zoo. The property is owned by the city, but the zoo is basically association-run and free from politics; most important, it is nonprofit, which helps bring in corporate dollars—providing somebody finds the donors. That somebody is usually me.

A big reality today is that the zoo business has taken on the "theme park" atmosphere. There's no getting around that. Walt Disney set the standard, and that's what people want. By this, I don't just mean having Mickey Mouse and Donald Duck running around; I mean cleanliness, friendliness, outstanding people who work for you, clean exhibits, that sort of thing. All those qualities we didn't have when I was hired; all those standards we now expect as routine, thanks to the hard work by many people. Some people even tell me the zoo doesn't smell anymore, but I wouldn't go quite that far.

Every year in the theme park business, you put in a new ride or attraction to get the visitors to come back. In the zoo business, we don't have the kind of money to put in a new animal exhibit each year—you're talking millions of dollars. But every two or three years, you better have something new at your zoo. I can always count on each spring's new animal births to boost attendance, but any new animal (like the panda) or a spectacular new exhibit will all but guarantee you a successful season. In the meantime, you do little things that keep people coming to the zoo.

Almost every weekend from April through September, there's some sort of promotion at the Columbus Zoo. It might be Symphony Day, with the Columbus Symphony Orchestra playing at the zoo. It might be the Columbus Ballet Met performing *Swan Lake* or animal-theme numbers specially choreographed and costumed for the zoo appearance. It might be Arts Day, with forty artists at their booths to show animal-related creations. It might be a birthday party for the twin gorillas, or any other animal. It might be the Zoo Run, which in 1988 brought three thousand runners to the zoo on a mid-October morning. Or Health, Fitness and Safety Day, on which thirty-some local agencies and organizations promote their programs, or Earth Day, when the conservation groups gather to educate the public.

It might be Teddy Bear Day, when every child who brings a teddy bear gets in free; we have volunteers dressed as nurses with stethoscopes giving every teddy a physical and giving its owner a little health certificate saying that teddy passed the test, that he's fine. It might be Christmas with the Animals, when kids bring food for the animals— fresh food, we check it all at the gate—and they get in free.

It might be the elephant tug-of-war, with Belinda pulling against a team of DJs from a radio station or against the offensive line of the Ohio State football team (Belinda wins every time; it's no contest). It might be—even if this has nothing to do with animals—Banana Split Day, when they build the world's largest banana split for the *Guinness Book of Records*. It might be a Halloween Party, Boo at the Zoo. Sailboat Days, ice-cream-eating contests, antique car shows.

The beat goes on and on—that's what the zoo is all about, or at least what zoo promotion is all about. We can't sit still, and I've never been able to anyway.

∧∧

Some of my schemes are harebrained, I'm the first to admit it. I think it's my enthusiasm that gets me carried away. Then by the time I realize a mistake's been made, it's too late—like in the case of the Great Zucchini.

The zoo's attendance for 1978 was a dismal 341,000— pretty lousy for a community of more than one million people. I didn't feel personally responsible, since I'd only been there a few months, but I wanted to start my first "zoo season," spring-summer of 1979, off with a bang. The opening of the outdoor gorilla habitat was nice, but now I wanted to add something commercial to attract the public.

One of my favorite acts at Ringling Brothers was the one where a guy gets shot out of a cannon into a net all the way across the arena. I'd read about the act, "The Great Zucchini," in a trade magazine, and I thought this might be just the kind of "bang" I was looking for. So I called a carnival and asked how I could get in touch with the Great Zucchini. They gave me the name of his agent, and before I knew it, I had a date for a cannon shot in May.

The local media were alerted, and I told them all about how I was going to have the Great Zucchini shot from a cannon to open the season (we're open 365 days a year, but it's always good to have a special opener for the summer season). The plan was to have this human cannonball go flying across the entrance lake and land in a big net in front of the zoo.

The day before the daredevil was supposed to arrive, my secretary came into my office to tell me that the Great Zucchini was here, that he'd just pulled up in his truck. I was puzzled as to why he was here early, but I was anxious to meet him. The moment I saw him standing there in the parking lot, I knew something might be wrong.

The truck was an old '52 pickup with a dirty metal cannon on top (the act I'd seen in the circus had a huge truck, easily thirty feet longer, with a much bigger, gleaming cannon mounted on top). There was no assistant, no beautiful girl in tights, no agent, no entourage—just a guy in overalls, standing by his truck, smoking a cigarette outside my zoo.

"How are you?" he said in a thick accent. "I'm the Great Zucchini."

"I'm Jack Hanna, from the Columbus Zoo."

We talked a little, and I told him that if he didn't mind, we'd get the media up here and we'd do a preliminary run. This was Friday, and I figured with a few calls to the TV stations I could get something on the evening news. (One thing I always try to do in the zoo business is to break an event—an animal birth, anything—on Thursday or Friday.

Even if the animal is born on Sunday, I try to keep it secret until Thursday or Friday so people will visit the zoo over the weekend. Of course, some of these jokers in the media are always saying, "Jack, we know it wasn't born on Thursday morning," but they'll usually go along.)

The press and TV people showed up, along with a few trustees, and in the meantime, the human cannonball pulled me aside and let me know that he wasn't going to pull the trigger on the cannon now, because it would take all the suspense out of his act for the next day. He had a point, but I had all these people there who wanted to see the shot. I told them he was going to practice—I just didn't say what.

Zucchini himself told the press that he was only going to lift the barrel and simulate what happens and that they could have pictures of him crawling out of the barrel or sitting up on the end of it. By this time, Zucchini had changed into his striped rocket suit that was all full of holes, and he was wearing an old beat-up World War I leather aviator hat with weird goggles. Now I was trying to keep him *away* from the press.

Well, if I'd thought anything was a little off before, I knew it for sure when Zucchini asked me, told me, to be his assistant working the cannon. He took me underneath the truck and showed me the controls, these big levers that I had to pull.

"Pull this one to make it go up, this one to make it go sideways, this one to make it go down," he told me.

It was dark, filthy and greasy down there, and I didn't know what I was doing. I also couldn't see what he was doing up above; I was supposed to react to his commands.

"Okay," he yelled. I could barely hear him. Was he down in the barrel? I pulled one lever and heard this whirring sound. Then I heard "Stop!" So I stopped. "Get ready," he yelled. The next move was to pull another lever, just a little bit, to make it go sideways. I heard "Okay" again. So I pulled. Then I heard this awful crash. Next I heard Dave Bricker saying, "Oh no!"

"What's wrong? What happened?" I asked Bricker from under all the machinery.

"Zucchini just fell off the cannon and went through the windshield of his truck."

"What do I do with the cannon? Should I move any more levers, do you think?" I asked him.

"Leave it all alone."

I came out from under the truck, and I saw broken glass all over the ground. The TV cameras were rolling and Zucchini was lying halfway through the broken windshield. Miraculously, he wasn't cut, but he was groaning—his aviator hat had blown off. Somehow he had slipped off the end of the barrel and fallen some fifteen feet down into the windshield.

"I'm all right," he moaned.

I couldn't believe it. This guy's the daredevil, and he goes and falls off the damn cannon before it even shoots. I'd already given him a $500 deposit on $2,000 and I hadn't gotten a thing for it.

The press people wanted to know what was going on, so I told them Zucchini was all right (I really didn't know—he said he was); I had to tell them something. "He'll be going on tomorrow," I told them; I didn't know that either.

I walked over to Mel Dodge, who was standing with the other trustees.

"He's not going off here," said Mel. "We'd have a lawsuit."

"Mel, we've got to do something." I had this thing all announced, all planned for opening day.

"Jack, he can't even get in his cannon," said Mel. "The guy'll land across the lake and kill somebody."

I had an idea. After checking with Mel, I went over to the amusement park next to the zoo and asked the owner if he'd like to have the Great Zucchini, free. It wasn't on zoo property, but it was right next to it. I knew attendance was terrible over there, and I made up some story about how we couldn't do it at the zoo because of the trees and everything.

The Great Zucchini ... I thought. Not all my promotions took off. (Columbus Zoo, Rick Prebeg)

"I need to get him over to your place to get him shot out of the cannon," I told him. "We'll pay for everything, no problem."

"You got it, Jack," the guy said. I don't think he knew what was happening, and I'm sure he didn't watch the news that night.

About 2,500 people showed up over there the next day— by no means a great turnout, but at least we had something. I had to practically beg Zucchini to go on, but I must say, he pulled himself together pretty well—I think he was a little embarrassed about his "practice" fall. He had some little speakers and some music, but he still didn't have anyone helping him. He set the net up what seemed like miles away, and I was really worried about how this would come out.

"Five, four, three, two, one . . ." Zucchini shouted from inside the cannon. My heart stopped. Zucchini pulled his trigger somewhere down in there, that ol' cannon rattled and with a huge BA-BOOM and a cloud of smoke, the human cannonball went flying through the air about fifty yards and plunked down in the middle of the net. Bull's-eye. I was very relieved, because I wasn't sure he knew what he was doing. I had just wanted to get this thing over with.

Afterward, when I went to shake his hand, I had to ask him something.

"By the way," I said, "when I saw you at Ringling Brothers, that truck was a lot longer and the cannon was all chrome and polished. Did you have to sell it or something?"

"No," he said, looking kind of sheepish. "I might as well tell you. I'm not the Great Zucchini—I'm his cousin."

For all I knew, he was probably his fifth or sixth cousin, but at least he hadn't killed anybody and his cannon didn't explode. That's all I cared about.

∧∧

Probably the greatest fund-raiser my first year at the zoo was Emily the chimp. Mel Dodge purchased Emily from the Cleveland Zoo for something like $2,500; in two years, she helped us raise nearly $200,000.

Emily was trained by Skip Butts, a young keeper who was currently working with sea lions. Before the Cleveland Zoo, Emily had lived with a family but they had to give her up because she was too destructive. Skip did a good job, but it took him about three months just to calm her down enough to be able to take her out in public. Once she caught on, she was a real ham.

Skip taught Emily to roller-skate, to ride a bike, to eat with silverware, to wear clothes—in short, all the things that drive some of my colleagues in the zoo world nuts. I respect their opinion, and I understand their point about not wanting to "humanize" animals. Today, we would not train a chimp in such fashion. But Emily was also an ambassador for her cousins, all the animals at the Columbus

Zoo. It was her entertaining, "humanized" personality that enabled us to raise money for the others.

If Mel and I couldn't manage to get an appointment with the CEO of a bank or corporation, we'd take Emily over to that man's office with a note in her hands. The note would say something like "Would you please help the Columbus Zoo?" It never failed, Emily would walk away with ten, fifteen thousand bucks at a whack.

One time we were in a bank president's office when she crapped all over the guy's rug. She was supposed to be toilet-trained, but once a chimp, always a chimp, right? Anyway, the gentleman wasn't amused, even if he did fork over a check for five grand. It was almost like "Here, take this check—just get out of here with that monkey."

Emily became quite a veteran of the banquet circuit, but like most chimps, she got ornery as she got older, and her days as a cute little animal gradually ended. It's a hormonal change chimpanzees go through, and it makes them very aggressive. So Emily went back to living the normal zoo animal's life.

Our next chimp ambassador was a beautiful infant named Sheba, whom we got from a research center when she was five months old. Marsha King, who now works in our herbivore-carnivore area, was hired to raise this little ape at home. Marsha was a tyrant where Sheba was concerned and I respected her for it. She was fanatical about Sheba's diet and care, picky about her volunteer babysitters (essential when you are home rearing a baby ape) and very professional and cautious during public appearances. Except for a diaper, Sheba didn't wear clothes and didn't do stunts or tricks. She was an all-natural chimp, and people loved her.

Sheba and Marsha made dozens of appearances with me, and logged hundreds of miles around central Ohio on their own, visiting schools, nursing homes and many other groups. They appeared on television several times and magazine articles were written about them. On warm weekend afternoons, they could be found parked on a shady, fenced-off area of the zoo grounds educating our visitors about chimpanzees. We'll never be able to calculate the effect that meeting Sheba had on people, but I do know that she touched many people's lives and that they came away with a better understanding of wildlife as a result.

Today, Sheba is at the Primate Cognition Project at Ohio State with Drs. Sally Boysen and Gary Berntson. Her progress there has been incredible, and she is well on her way to shattering current notions about the intelligence of our nearest relative in the animal world.

Mel Dodge has always been a tremendous fund-raiser; he loves to take animals out to the public. Getting the donations was one thing, but Mel also got a big kick out of surprising people, out of being a practical joker.

Every Christmas, Mel and I take an animal around to the offices of the various people who've made donations during the year. We thank them for their help and support, and we have pictures taken of them with a baby lion, a baby elephant, whatever. People don't forget that—we're not there to ask for money, we're there to thank them.

One year, Mel and I were going around with a full-grown camel. In the middle of our appointed rounds, we happened to be driving by the Capitol. Mel turned to me—we were in a zoo truck—and said, "Let's stop in and see the governor."

"Mel, we don't have an appointment," I said, as if we could bring a camel up to see Governor Rhodes with an appointment.

"Don't worry about it," he said. "Let's go see him."

We got out of the truck, and Mel pulled the camel out of the back. We started up the steps to the Capitol; he was leading, I was trailing, cleaning up the mess. The state troopers stopped us at the entrance, but the governor's secretary called down and said it was all right.

Of course, I figured Mel knew the governor, but I didn't know how well or how much the governor wanted to have a visit from a camel. (Governor James Rhodes was about to leave office after four terms.)

*M*onkey see, monkey do. Teak and Amber already had theirs.
(Earl W. Smith, III)

*W*e treat our zoo babies with great care. This tiny orange tiger, will weigh about four to five hundred pounds when full grown. (Columbus Zoo, Nancy Staley)

*E*veryone has fun at the zoo.
(Pat Asher)

*J*ulie and a chimp named Emily monkeying around.
(Greg Miller)

*M*osuba and Macombo II when they were about a month old.
(Columbus Zoo, Rick Preburg)

*J*oan Lunden and I with a tall friend during her visit to the zoo.
(Pat Asher)

*B*ottom: *From the moment we got to Columbus, the zoo has been a big part of our family life.* (Columbus Zoo, Susan Scherer)

*S*ome people would say the zoo's our whole life now. (Columbus Zoo, Rick Preberg)

We decorate the zoo for holidays throughout the year—Christmas is one of the most beautiful. (Columbus Zoo, Nancy Staley)

When we got up there, the secretary said, "Mr. Dodge, the governor is in his final cabinet meeting right now. If you'd like to wait . . ."

"That's no problem," Mel said, pushing the door open before the secretary could stop him.

We got in there, and Governor Rhodes looked up without smiling, like this kind of thing went on every day. His cabinet members were in hysterics, but I was fearful for my job. Mel was about to retire; I was just getting started.

"Governor," said Mel, "we've just come by to pay our respects and thank you on behalf of the Columbus Zoo."

"Why, thank you, Mel," said the governor, "but I believe you're on the wrong end of the camel."

∧∧

In the early spring of 1980, after a typically lousy late winter, I wanted to do an Easter promotion to get the kids back out to the zoo. An Easter egg hunt is nothing new as far as promotion goes, but I thought it would be a natural, a nice thing to usher in the spring season.

Mel warned me not to do it. "It takes a lot of organization, a lot of planning, Jack," he said. "A lot of things can go wrong. I wouldn't do it."

I told him we weren't getting people in the springtime, and that even if the weather wasn't great, Easter is special and an egg hunt would bring the people out. Mel wouldn't deny that, but he still insisted he wouldn't do it. I should have listened to him.

We ordered about 1,500 marshmallow-filled chocolate eggs, and I announced the event in the papers and on the radio. I said I was going to give big prizes to those who could find the first twelve eggs (I got adult volunteers to hide all the eggs). There were many major screw-ups with this thing, but one of the main ones was not giving every kid a prize. Another one was not dividing the kids into age groups. In addition, I didn't expect a very large crowd because the weather forecast predicted a rainy, cold day.

Anyway, on the day of the hunt, a beautiful, sunny pre-Easter Saturday, kids and their parents started coming to the zoo earlier than ever before. Dave Bricker called me over the radio about 9 A.M. to tell me there were three to four hundred people outside the gates (the zoo didn't open until ten; the hunt was scheduled for eleven). I said that was great, tremendous. I remember being really excited, pumped up by the gorgeous weather. And of course all these kids are jumping up and down and screaming—they were excited just to be out.

A half hour later, Bricker called to tell me there were now about a thousand people gathered at the gate; he said we'd better open early. Nowhere near all the people had arrived, and I completely forgot I only had 1,500 eggs. I was still very excited about the big turnout.

So we let everybody in, and we took them all down along the river to this acre-and-a-half area where we had the eggs hidden. There were about a dozen volunteer docents helping and just a single rope around the area. We had Gabe Ritter, a nice man (and a sucker like me) who likes to play the Easter Bunny and lead all the kids in a bunny hop. Around the zoo, I saw all the kids hopping to the music, and I still thought, this is great—not knowing what was going to happen.

By ten-thirty there were almost three thousand people there, and we could barely hold them back from the ropes. I began to see the danger. The kids were going nuts, dying to get at those chocolate eggs, and the parents were doing little to control them. We knew we had to start this thing soon.

I picked up my bullhorn to start the countdown, but before I could even count to one, a couple of parents and their kids came through the ropes. That started a mass stampede, and within thirty seconds there wasn't one egg left. In fact, there wasn't anything left—it was like they'd sucked up the earth.

It was a terrible scene. Everywhere kids were crying because they hadn't gotten even one egg. One kid's ear was cut—he had blood all over his face; another had a black eye. A local ABC news crew was rolling and getting it all on film.

All of a sudden people came toward me. Who was responsible for this? Who can we blame for this mess? They didn't have far to look. One mother grabbed me by the shirt and ripped the epaulets off my safari shirt. "I can't believe you're this dumb, that you'd have an Easter egg hunt for all these kids without enough eggs," she yelled at me. I couldn't believe it either.

Bricker escorted me back to my office, and I asked him to announce over the bullhorn that we'd give every kid who didn't get an egg or a prize a free pass to the zoo. We were there for hours handing out free passes.

That night Mel called me at home.

"What'd I tell you?" he said, but he didn't rub it in. Mel is right 99 percent of the time. He laughed about it a little, which was good, because I felt terrible.

I was almost asleep when the phone rang again. It was a guy from the Associated Press wanting to know what happened. I didn't mind and I knew I couldn't run away from the incident, but I shouldn't have spoken my mind.

"You wouldn't think that the adults would go out and hunt eggs," I told him. "It was like watching five thousand rats that haven't eaten in weeks."

The next day everybody was in an uproar reading about how the Columbus Zoo director called the people of Columbus rats. Then Paul Harvey came on with it on his radio show, went through the whole friggin' story. I didn't think I'd ever live it down.

The next year, we had another Easter egg hunt; I was determined to do it right. We got 5,000 eggs, and it rained—I had to eat or give away 4,500 eggs. The following year, I had 5,000 eggs, it was 85 degrees and they all melted—the ants got in them.

Today we have the Easter egg scene very well organized. The kids go to stations throughout the zoo where a hundred volunteers hand out little surprises like chocolate eggs and

Easter coloring books. Everybody gets something. I learned
the hard way—I always do, and I hate Easter eggs to this
day.

⋀⋀

As for bonehead plays, no chapter would be complete
without the infamous Great Wallenda episode. This was
actually a very successful promotion—it brought 15,000
people out to the zoo—but it failed for me personally, by
bringing practically the entire zoo community down on my
head. Yes, I was in the wrong, though I didn't realize it at
the time.

The Great Wallendas were the greatest aerial act in the
world. In 1980, the grandfather, Carl Wallenda, fell to his
death in a high-wire accident in Puerto Rico. Since then,
the family had fallen on hard times; people were leery of
booking them. But in the spring of 1982, I read an article
that Enrico, the grandson, was trying to make a comeback.
I found out he would be touring the area, so I thought,
hey, why not have him perform his act over some wild
animals at the zoo?

I wrote Enrico Wallenda with my proposal, and he got
back to me saying he loved the idea, and that he loved zoos
and animals.

"The Wallendas like to do dramatic things," he told me
when we first met here in Ohio. "We have walked across
canyons, gorges, waterfalls, tall buildings." Now he said he
wanted to walk above the lions, tigers and gorillas.

We settled on a price and a date, and once again I
announced my plan to the papers. I also emphasized the
fact that with cutbacks in federal funding, we needed more
promotions.

Wallenda told one newspaper that he was going to toss a
banana to Bongo the gorilla to get his attention. Of course,
Bongo, who'd never seen people in the air before, wouldn't
need much to get his attention. The same article mentioned
that police teams and an ambulance would be there—a "just
in case" kind of thing. It didn't sound right, and I knew this
wasn't the way we wanted to go—not with the gorillas.

The next day my great-apes people came to me with grave concerns. We talked, and they told me they feared for the safety of the animals, and were worried about how the stunt might trivialize the gorilla collection at the zoo, as well as those of other zoos. I agreed with them; I'm not all promotion-oriented. But I still wanted Wallenda, so we agreed to do it over the tigers. My mistake, or one of them, was not respecting the tigers in the same way.

*B*onehead Promotion Number Two—the Great Wallenda.
(*Columbus Dispatch*, Fred Shannon)

Wallenda put on a great show for the crowds that came to the zoo; he's not just an aerialist, he's a performer. He about gave me a heart attack when he faked his fall over the tiger pit. (He gave my wife and me lessons afterward on a wire two feet off the ground, and I couldn't get three feet without falling off.)

I really felt quite confident about Enrico, or I wouldn't have done the show. We did have some police standing by. The tigers didn't seem to be bothered—they growled every so often like they always do. A reporter asked me what I would have done had Wallenda fallen into the pit. I couldn't really answer that, since Enrico had expressly stated that he did not want the animals harmed under any circumstances. ·

Several days later, I heard it big-time from the executive director of the American Association of Zoological Parks and Aquariums, Robert Wagner. Wagner is a good man, a serious man, and he explained to me what I had done wrong according to AAZPA ethics. With the act, I had exploited the Bengal tigers.

It was related to showmanship, not to zookeeping, and could have resulted in the uncalled-for injury or death to either performer or animal. I apologized, and I really did feel bad about my unprofessional behavior, about going outside the standards of zookeeping. But I must admit, deep down inside, I was still thrilled about all those people we drew. Today, I would rather have no visitors than put on a stunt like that again.

Wallenda felt bad for all the heat I took. He wrote to tell me he never would have done it if he had known I would get into trouble. I always thought he was a classy guy. A nice postscript to the incident as far as he's concerned was his marriage to the reporter who first interviewed him in Columbus. Within a year, he had her walking the high wire, and today she performs in his act. But now, when they come to perform in Columbus, instead of seeing them at the zoo, we always go see them in the circus.

⋀⋀

My friend Pepè and I—a successful zoo promotion. (Columbus Zoo file)

Since I've become known around Columbus, I've lent my name to a few products in order to get zoo donations. People see me in pictures for car ads with a lot of zoo animals all around and think I make tons of money from it. I don't. The whole purpose is to get a free truck along with corporate donations for the zoo.

The single largest promotional campaign that I've ever been involved with was the Kroger grocery chain frozen-food promotion. It all began when some of their people approached me saying they wanted to tie me in to a frozen-food campaign with a mascot penguin. I said fine, what's in it for the zoo? They said, what do you need? Two hundred and fifty thousand dollars toward an exhibit for visiting giant pandas in 1992, I told them. No problem, they said.

One of my close friends at Kroger, Dave Tebay, came up with an idea for TV commercials in which Pepè the Penguin had a secret that he was keeping from me. In the commercials, I was constantly looking for Pepè, who was hiding from me—in a frozen-food truck, in a warehouse, at the airport, wherever (we used a tame penguin for the ads). The secret the first year was that Pepè had a donation for the zoo and that this would be announced on a special date. I had to sign affidavits that I wouldn't tell anyone I knew what it was, and I didn't, not even Suzi.

Kroger also pulled off a great coup when they got Vice President George Bush to announce Pepè's secret in a sixty-second spot filmed in Washington, D.C. Congressman Chalmers Wylie is a friend of Bush's and asked him to do it for the zoo; naturally, there was no mention of Kroger, just that Pepè was giving all that dough to the zoo to build a panda exhibit for 1992. He also said that the pandas represented the bettering of relations between the people of the United States and the people of China.

My problem, then, was that the pandas were not a sure thing. We're supposed to have them in 1992, but the Chinese have experienced a great deal of international controversy with their "leasing" of animals, especially the pandas, to Western zoos. Kroger said no problem, that I could do something else at the zoo with the money. They had already sold an extra six million bags of frozen food from the promotion, so I guess they were happy. How about a $250,000 cockroach exhibit?

Pepè's secret the next year was that he was giving out 250,000 bags of food to the needy. Again, I was in these commercials, always looking for Pepè. I knew it was a good cause, and at the same time it kept the zoo in the spotlight, but it was starting to get tiresome.

Everywhere I went, people yelled Pepè this, Pepè that. It was like my whole life revolved around a penguin that didn't even exist. When the campaign had a new twist, "Help Jack find Pepè," I started getting calls from drunks in the middle of the night: "Pepè's in the toilet." I received loads of nasty letters from people who thought Pepè was obnoxious. I even got short with people who asked about Pepè. "I barbecued him," I'd tell them.

That's the power of television. I put in a great deal of work on this Pepè thing, never realizing how closely identified with the product I would become. Once they "found" Pepè, people began to leave me alone. But we not only received the money for the zoo from this, we received a lot of free publicity, and for that I'm always grateful, especially to Kroger.

Promotions can be serious or silly. Successful or bombs. Good ideas or bad ideas. What I do know is that they serve a number of purposes, including bringing more people through the gate, most of whom have a good time, come back again, buy a membership, adopt an animal or in some other way benefit the zoo.

Promotions also allow businesses to provide community service through their sponsorships and donations, thus benefiting the zoo and themselves. They also provide avenues for other community organizations to promote their programs and services during our "theme" days—Earth Day, Health, Fitness and Safety Day, Arts Day and so on. Some of these events become family traditions that are anticipated year after year, especially Christmas with the Animals, Symphony Day and our Halloween and Easter celebrations. Serious or silly, promotions prove the point that there's something for everyone at the zoo.

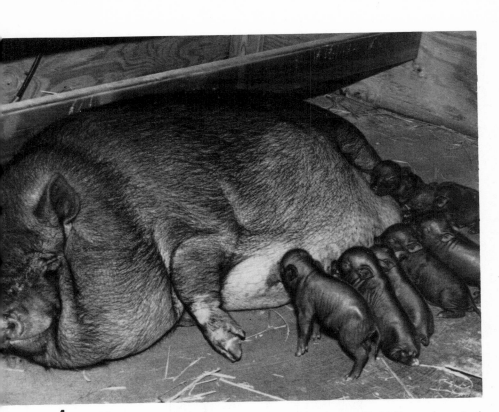

A Vietnamese pot-bellied pig with her piglets. Even low-profile births are important.
(Columbus Zoo, Nancy Staley)

12

ZOO BIRTHS

The birth of any animal is probably the single most rewarding side to being a zoo director. In a sense, it's like being a grandfather: you can just sit back most of the time, appreciate and enjoy. Not a week goes by without an important birth—and they're all important—happening at the zoo.

Anyone who knows the zoo business also knows that newborns are great attractions. Naturally, "high-profile" animals like gorillas, lions and elephants receive top billing from the press and the public, but around here we're tickled with each and every birth, from cougar to cockroach, from hippo to hyena.

One reason our births captivate the public so much is the anthropomorphizing of animals. Whether the "purists" in the zoo field like it or not, zoo animals take on character in the public eye. After the average patron has visited the zoo two or three times in one summer, certain animals become favorites, become family. The zoo visitor feels like he knows the animal, and in his own way, he does. When the animal has a baby—and zoo patrons are kept informed by newsletters, television, newspapers, etc.—it becomes a big family event.

But most of all, zoo births are a means toward continuing propagation and the preservation of many species. Breeding has become an all-important activity in zoos, if not the most important. It's what we're here for. We don't want to sit around and watch Clyde the rhino die in a cage after forty years, then go out to the Serengeti Plain in Africa and net another rhino. Thank goodness those days are over. We want to make a lot of little Clydes.

In some cases, the captive birth of an animal takes on worldwide significance, especially if you're talking about endangered species. You've got more tigers living in zoos on this planet than you have in the wild; they can breed in captivity. There are but a handful of black rhinos left in Africa—whether or not they can be propagated in zoos could determine the fate of their species.

*Z*ero with her baby, Icee, in their den. They stayed in the den from the birth in November until April. (Columbus Zoo, Lyle Holbrook)

With any captive birth of an endangered animal, the public becomes better educated and more conscious of that species' struggle for survival. Everybody knows about the giant pandas' problem, and there have been only a few born in zoos worldwide.

But getting down to basic sentimentality, baby animals are cute, and there's no denying it. They look especially appealing when they're little and playful, even if they're guaranteed to become ugly when they're older. A polar bear cub or a baby elephant will draw crowds. That's why one of the most gratifying sounds to me is to hear the people crowding around a newborn animal going, "Awwwwww."

∧∧

When is or isn't an elephant pregnant? You'd think we'd be able to know these things, being in the zoo business and all, but it's not that simple. If it were, then I wouldn't have suffered yet another embarrassing episode in my zoo career. The bummer with this one was that it lasted so long.

Very little is known about Asian elephants, since there are so few of them born in captivity. We had high hopes for Bomba, one of our resident female pachyderms, but in the long run, she let us down—and it was a long run.

We first bred Bomba to Koko in the summer of 1979— we thought. It's hard to see what they're doing, they're so damn big; also, like most people and most animals, elephants aren't particularly thrilled to get things going while being watched. My keepers thought the two had mated— in any case, they looked like they were doing something. Later we realized that maybe they didn't mate when we thought, but my keepers thought they may have mated eight months after that. So we were confused from the start.

Adding to the confusion was the fact that an elephant's gestation period is variable. It is generally twenty-two months, but it can come in at twenty or stretch out to twenty-four or twenty-five months.

*H*ere I am with Boomer and Belle, our baby African elephants, both age two. At birth the babies weighed two hundred pounds and can grow to be over 5 tons.
(Columbus Zoo, Nancy Staley)

About sixteen or seventeen months after we thought Bomba had mated with Koko, she began to put on weight and her appetite increased. Given that we thought she'd mated, it was a reasonable deduction that she might be pregnant, but there was nobody to say for sure. We called the people in Portland, who successfully bred elephants, and they told us, "You'll know it for sure when she's expecting—she'll be huge." And she was.

I brought in three of the very best obstetricians in town to examine her. At first they tried human pregnancy tests, but that didn't work. Dr. James "Nick" Baird (who also happens to be my wife's gynecologist) stuck his arm up there to the shoulder, but he couldn't get anywhere near where the amniotic sac ought to be.

The doctors then suggested we try ultrasound, which I thought was a good idea. I was a little worried about what my elephant might do to the expensive equipment, but Bomba was pretty quiet and let herself be examined. Still, the tests proved inconclusive. The problem was that the elephant's skin was much too thick for the sound waves to penetrate.

Meanwhile, Ted Spellmire, head pachyderm keeper, had done his own test based on an Indian veterinary manual. The test involved injecting the blood from a female elephant into the bloodstream of a male frog. If the frog develops sperm (from its hormones being disturbed), it means the elephant is pregnant. This is actually a hormone test, which I later found out was an old pregnancy test for humans. Anyway, sure enough, the frog developed sperm, so Bomba was supposed to be pregnant.

A couple months later, the doctors returned with a more powerful ultrasound unit, and this time their testing showed what they thought was the vertebrae of a baby elephant. But it was a shadowy outline at best, so nobody wanted to make it definite. We actually ran the ultrasound photo in our newsletter, pointing out the spine!

My problem, as well as everyone else's, was that we really wanted this baby. We wanted Bomba to be pregnant. After the first gorilla born in captivity, after the rare cheetah births, we wanted to add to the Columbus Zoo's accomplishments a rare Asian elephant birth. I should have waited to announce her pregnancy, but as usual, I didn't. Besides, according to that Indian manual, she was pregnant, and they had to know more about elephants than we did. So I let it out to the media that Bomba was going to have a baby.

When twenty-five months had gone by, I started getting worried again. Bomba had been gaining weight all along, but she was eating so darn much and we kept feeding her, so that didn't have to mean anything at all. I thought maybe she was taking us for a ride. She obviously enjoyed the special treatment she was receiving—she was like the queen of the zoo, and she knew it.

Around Christmas 1981—we were now working off the second mating date—I was telling people that she was definitely overdue but that we could expect a baby any day now. People were stopping me and calling all the time. This thing was like a wart, getting very annoying to me.

At about that same time, we'd had volunteers doing an around-the-clock pregnancy watch for a couple of months. This was my idea, since the birth was so important. They were all very excited about it; everybody wanted to be the one on duty when Bomba dropped the big one. And that's why I got a false alarm in the middle of one night. She wasn't having a baby; she was going to the bathroom. Several of the volunteers were all over the papers giving interviews, which of course was their right. None of us really knew what was going on anyway.

Zoo volunteers are an important part of our breeding program; they vigilantly watch, keep a logbook and take notes during the night hours, which is when many of the animals give birth. Most of the viewing is done by remote television monitors, and for the most part, it's tedious work. If anything should happen, they've been well trained to alert the keepers and the veterinarian.

We also have the capability to videotape during the animal watch, and we save the footage for future reference in special pregnancies, like that of a rare elephant. This got so expensive, I had to have a video store donate tapes (the local television affiliates loaned us the cameras). Even then, after I don't know how many hundreds of hours, we had to erase and start over. We would have needed a new building just to store the damn tapes.

Meanwhile, my buddies at the Columbus *Citizen-Journal* were having a ball with Bomba's "pregnancy." I didn't object when they started a "guess the birth date" contest. I even put up a lifetime family zoo membership to add to their $100 prize. What the hell, might as well get some publicity out of this. But I was getting pretty nervous that we might be jinxing the whole thing.

A few more months of nothin' doin', and we had a big question mark on our hands. Now she'd been pregnant for, what, thirty-two months? We knew that wasn't possible, or was it? It seemed like nobody wanted to go out on a limb and say she wasn't pregnant. I couldn't blame my OBs. Dr. Baird is a good friend and a great doctor, but he didn't go to med school to treat elephants.

Christmas 1982—still nothing. I had to make some kind of decision, and that's when we thankfully closed up shop on Bomba, not a moment too soon. I didn't know what happened (I still don't), and that's what I announced. I didn't know why she'd gained seven hundred pounds (aside

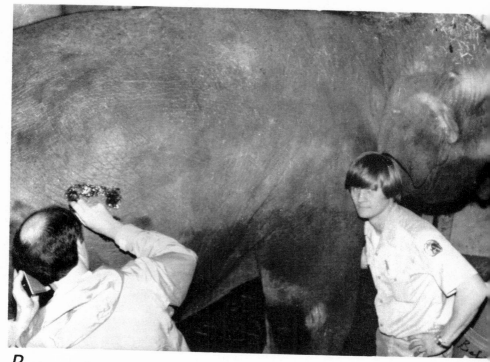

*B*omba gets ultrasound. (Columbus Zoo file)

from the fact that we overfed her), I didn't know why the doctors might have seen an elephant fetus, I didn't know why my keepers thought they saw her mate. She might have had a tumor, she might have had a false pregnancy, she might have been pregnant and reabsorbed the fetus— what she and we didn't have was an elephant breeding expert on hand. We sure could have used one. After more than three years, Bomba bombed.

∧∧

When a gorilla becomes pregnant here at the zoo, we go to great lengths to ensure the well-being of the animal and her future offspring. People used to think we were crazy putting the pregnant female down (anesthetizing), but it's the only way to examine her. The information we learn not only tells us whether she and the fetus are all right or not; just as in humans, it helps pinpoint the birth date. Then we can start our gorilla watches accordingly, a few weeks ahead of the due date.

Back in the summer of 1983, we were doing a typical exam on Bridgette, the gorilla on breeding loan from the Henry Doorly Zoo in Omaha. Present were the ape staff, our veterinarian Dr. Harrison Gardner, Dr. Nick Baird and, for the first time, Dr. Larry Stempel, who was administering the sonogram. After shaving Bridgette's belly, Dr. Stempel began scanning with his instrument, watching the monitor. He'd barely been at it a minute when he stopped suddenly.

"I can't believe this," he said. "Take a picture," he told his assistant. "Take another one . . . one more." He was very intent and seemed excited. None of us knew what was happening.

"Dr. Stempel, what's going on?" I asked. "Is the baby dead?"

"No," he said, and continued scanning. After a minute or so, he looked up. "I think there's twins in there."

"Dr. Stempel," I said, "I don't know everything about gorillas, but I don't think twins have ever been born in captivity." (I found out later they had—twice, in Germany and Spain.) "Are you sure about this?"

"Is this guy for real?" asked head keeper Dianna Frisch. All the keepers were shaking their heads in disbelief.

Nick Baird went over to have a look at the monitor. "Looks like two heads to me," he said. "Could you back up a little, Larry? . . . Yes . . . there are definitely two gorillas there."

"Now, Nick," I said, "I'm going to announce this, and I'm not going to make a fool of myself." I was still thinking of Bomba. "Are both you guys willing to put your reputations on the line with this?"

"No problem, Jack," Nick said. "You've got twin gorillas there."

"And they're in perfect shape," added Dr. Stempel, who was measuring their size, heart rate, everything. Now we were all ecstatic with the news.

The twins were born a little after midnight on October 26, a night that my wife happened to be on gorilla watch. We had more than sixty volunteers watching Bridgette over the previous seven weeks, but that night someone phoned Suzi at the last minute to ask her to sub.

Suzi had a few tense moments. She didn't know how to start the video machine and she couldn't seem to work the walkie-talkie to call for help. She did, however, pick up on the most important thing, and that was that Bridgette was going into labor. A security officer heard her screaming into the walkie-talkie and came by to help out.

As always, all the vets, doctors and keepers were immediately summoned. I used to be called first, but since I'm no good to anybody, I tell them to call me last. At a little after midnight, Bridgette moved to her nesting area, and with one long, hard push, the first baby was born.

The critical thing was how quickly the second baby would be born, since we had no research, no precedent. Bridgette immediately picked up the first infant (Baby A), and fifty-seconds later the second baby (Baby B) was born. She leaned over to tend to this infant but became distracted by a cry from her firstborn. She started consuming the placenta (a natural and important process), meanwhile forgetting Baby B, who was still enclosed in the amniotic sac.

The doctors said we could wait about three minutes, then somebody would have to go in and get that baby out of the sac. But you can't just walk in on a full-grown gorilla.

Dianna coaxed Bridgette, who was cradling Baby A, to a back cage while the doctors rushed in and tore open the sac. There was Baby B, moving and breathing.

Nick Baird wrapped him in a blanket and headed out to the nursery, where incubators and staff were waiting. But Nick got lost in the zoo maintenance area and we had to go find him. What a scene it was, Nick lost in the dark holding a rare twin baby gorilla in a blanket.

We had to pull Baby A as well, since that was the request of his owner, the Henry Doorly Zoo. With such a high-profile birth, no one wanted to take any chances, and it's possible that Bridgette could not have handled two babies anyway. Dr. Gardner tranquilized Bridgette, and Dianna went in and grabbed the baby before the mother could fall on him.

The twins were boys, in beautiful condition, weighing in at four pounds eight ounces each. They both had long eyelashes, and little arms that were grabbing out at everything—they were winners, total knockouts.

Because the twins were the result of a breeding loan, after the ultrasound it had been decided between Dr. Lee Simmons, the Henry Doorly Zoo director, and myself that each zoo would own one twin, the firstborn going to Omaha and the second to Columbus. We eventually worked out an agreement whereby they traveled between Columbus and Omaha each year—about eight months in Columbus and four in Omaha—for the first four years.

It took months, but we finally got past "A" and "B" and named them Mosuba (for the three Columbus volunteers who helped raised them in the nursery-*Mo*lly, *Su*e and *Ba*rb) and Macombo II (for Colo's father, Baron Macombo).

Every year for their first four birthdays, we had a party for the twins on *Good Morning America*. In fact, their birth brought about my first appearance on the show. For the first four years, the boys and I had cake together on the air, but by 1988 they were about a hundred pounds each and very powerful, quite capable of jerking me around if they chose. I decided not to go in with them that year, but we wished them "happy birthday" on the air and did a program on how endangered gorillas are today.

It is quite possible that the twins would continue to get along throughout life, but even in the wild they might not choose to stay together. The Propagation Committee of the Species Survival Plan (SSP) of AAZPA has recommended to both zoos that the twins be separated when they reach maturity and integrated into unrelated family groups for genetic reasons. In the captive gorilla world, the gene pool we have now is all we will ever have (because we no longer take gorillas out of the wild), so genetic diversity is absolutely critical. We must make decisions about the twins based on what is best for them and the other captive gorillas in the world.

In the meantime, they're still very close to each other and doing great in a family group . . . learning all the gorilla rules and regulations. And that's a tough test to pass.

ᐱᐱ

Some births are less glamorous than others, but as I said before, they're never any less important. You probably wouldn't think much about a couple of turtles being born, unless you realized how rare they are. When two baby yellow-spotted side-neck turtles chewed their way through their eggshells on August 26, 1983, we were again making zoo history.

Mike Goode, Dan Badgley and the people in the reptile department have done a fantastic job over the years. In a five-year span, they managed to breed twenty-five different species of turtles—an unrivaled feat in the zoo world. And they never do it exactly by the book (whatever the book on reptiles or amphibians is). In the case of the turtles, they found that a diet of trout chow somehow increased fertility. The special care taken to create proper nesting areas plays a large part as well.

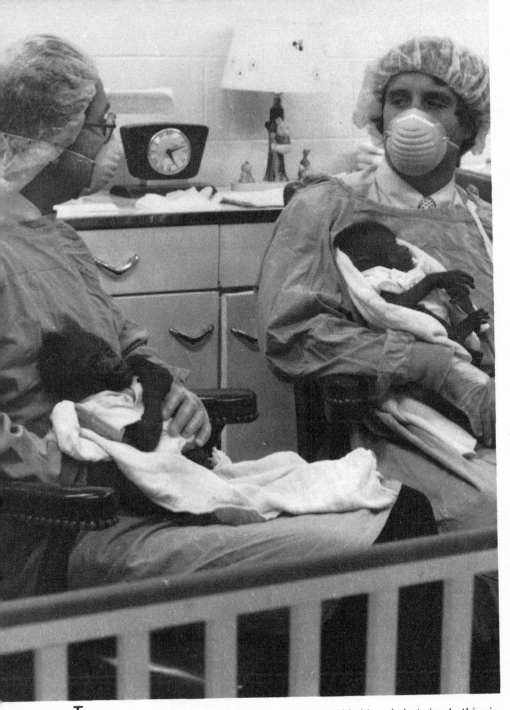

The proud fathers: Lee Simmons of the Omaha Zoo and I hold our baby twins. In this picture, they're a week old. (Columbus Zoo, Julie Estadt)

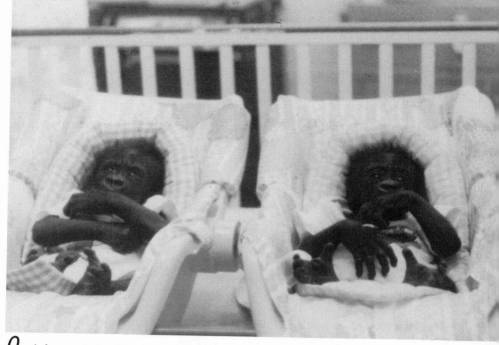

*O*ur infamous twins, Mosuba and Macombo II. (Columbus Zoo file)

*G*rowing boys. (Columbus Zoo, Joan Nease)

These South American turtles were the first of their species ever hatched in captivity (the eggs had been "dropped" two months earlier). They're endangered today because they'd been overexported in the past, as well as overeaten by Amazon natives. Hopefully, they'll make a comeback, and every little bit helps, right?

∧∧

Bill Cupps came to me on my second day at the zoo and told me we could breed cheetahs, an endangered species. I didn't pay much attention, because I knew it was very difficult. So I told him fine, let's do it. Today we have the largest cheetah collection in the United States and we are second in total numbers bred and still breeding, a credit to Bill, his staff and the veterinarians.

Bill is the head keeper of cheetahs and bears and the kind of worker anyone would want to have in any field. He's the strong, silent type—a doer not a talker. He never finished high school, and he started here as a keeper trainee and worked his way up. Today he gives lectures based on his knowledge of breeding, which he's gathered not from zoology textbooks but from years of on-the-job experience. And the job for Bill—like all dedicated zoo people—is a twenty-four-hour one.

When I was first getting to know my staff, Bill, like the others, was wary of my enthusiasm. He loved his animals, but he'd seen a lot of indifference since he'd been at the zoo. I think I proved myself to him one night when I overheard a call for help on the radio coming from the cheetah area. I ran back there and found Bill fighting off a big male cat. The female was trying to drag the babies out of harm's way, and some of them were dying. Together, we got the male out of there. I knew Bill appreciated it—not for his hide, but for the cubs.

Convincing cheetahs to breed in captivity is tricky business, but Bill has found an ingenious "productive" method. He separates the males from the females for about three to four weeks. Then around breeding time, he puts them back together in the same habitat and lets nature take its course. Absence always makes the heart grow fonder.

He will also feed five or six cheetahs together so that they have to compete for food. Competition with other males helps arouse the cheetah. A lot of scrapping goes on between the aggressive males, but eventually one will establish dominance and win the hearts of the females. And that's how we've wound up with ninety-four cheetah births in the past ten years.

Another fascinating zoo birth, partly because it's so difficult, partly because the animal is so savage, is the polar bear. Here again, we can thank Bill Cupps and his staff, who are all self-taught on this.

*C*olumbia with her three cheetah cubs. (*Columbus Citizen Journal*, Dick Garrett)

What they did was build a little birthing den, about eight feet square, in the back of the bear's cave. The bears mate in the late spring and eat a great deal through the summer and fall, fattening themselves up for the winter. At some point, usually in November, Bill waits for the right day and locks the female up in the den. We have a one-way window and infrared lighting to monitor the animal. At first, she paces and raises all kinds of Cain, but within a day or so she lies down and curls up. A few weeks later, she has her baby.

The mother lives off her fat and won't be fed from November until she comes out in March or April. She might have a little water, but she rarely even touches that. But the cubs are the most amazing things. Those little creatures weigh about fourteen ounces at birth—this is coming from an eight-hundred-pound animal. They look like little rats with no hair and just about fit in the palm of your hand. The videotape of mother and baby that we get through the one-way glass is mind-blowing—and beautiful.

In the spring, the mother brings the cub out, and it's a major, I mean *major* attraction. It'll weigh twelve to fifteen pounds, a snow-white little puffball. The mother lies outside on the rocks and puts that little cub up to her breast, and it's just a wonderful thing to see a creature so huge and so savage take care of such a delicate little baby that way. Each time we announce a polar bear birth it's the zoo's way of saying "spring is here."

A giraffe birth is one of the most nerve-wracking we have at the zoo, and at the same time one of the most rewarding. There are potential problems with giraffe births because the animal is so large and unwieldy and because the mother stands up while dropping her offspring four or five feet. That's right—the baby just drops from the mother, right to the ground. What a way to come into the world.

The baby giraffe is all neck and legs coming out. Eventually, like a newborn colt, it'll push on those skinny legs and just wiggle itself up—a joy to behold. With its big brown eyes, the baby giraffe is just about unequaled in the cuteness department. After a couple of days, all cleaned off, it gets all fluffy and looks like a big stuffed toy. Gorgeous.

Head keeper Dan Hunt and his herbivore-carnivore staff have done a terrific job of seeing that the giraffe births and all the others in their section are successful. Captive animals are often nervous at birth, and the keepers try to create a quiet atmosphere in which the mother is comfortable. They are respectful of her personality and her privacy.

∧∧

Eagle births are always critical, both in the wild and at the zoo; each and every successful hatching helps offset their well-known status as an endangered species. They always hatch in a nest on high, usually after an incubation of thirty-six days or so. During incubation, the parents will share sitting on the egg. The weather plays a large part in whether the eaglet survives once it's hatched. High winds and harsh spring weather can be fatal; meddling by humans can spook the parents into harming the offspring.

George and Georgina, our two Columbus Zoo bald eagles, were prolific parents. Georgina lived to be about twenty-five (she died in the summer of 1988) and hatched nine eaglets over a ten-year period. Of those, five survived, but one came through with flying colors. Freedom was born at the Columbus Zoo in 1982 and released in the Tennessee Valley before he could fly. Three years later, he himself bred in the wild and hatched an eaglet. That was a big first.

Giraffe births are among the most nerve-wracking, because the baby drops about 5 feet to the ground. Here Noinu cleans her minutes-old newborn.
(Columbus Zoo, Rick Prebeg)

Releasing such an endangered species into the wild is one of the greatest feelings to be experienced in all of the zoo business. In Freedom's case, Dick

*F*reedom, an American bald eagle, was born at the Zoo and released in the Tennessee Valley before he could fly. (Columbus Dispatch)

Pope, our curator of birds, first had to go into the caged habitat and net the mother before grabbing the baby, who was then six weeks old. Next the eaglet was transferred to a cage and taken to Tennessee, where he came under the Division of Wildlife's jurisdiction.

The bird was then taken to a hacking tower high above the tree line surrounding Norris Lake. The hacking tower is a boxlike apparatus that allows the bird to be fed (by means of a pulley from another tower) for a few weeks until it can fish and hunt on its own.

When the bird is old enough, it's released from the tower. This is a glorious moment. It'll take about a twenty-foot drop at first, then with a couple of wing flaps, it'll go soaring off against the sky. Just thinking about it gives me goose bumps.

The bald eagle is not just our national symbol. The bald eagle born in a zoo never officially belongs to that zoo, but remains the property of the federal government. When we release a captive-born bald eagle such as Freedom, it's a group effort involving zoo, state and federal agencies.

Freedom's release was part of a successful nationwide program (two years earlier, we had released an eaglet in upstate New York). We played our part by being one of a handful of zoos ever to breed eagles in captivity. Tennessee ecologists did their part by diligently tracking the birds and their offspring. Freedom played his part first by surviving—he was tagged before being released—then by finding a mate and reproducing. Today, he hunts and fishes over the Tennessee Valley in the grand fashion of our national bird.

Now, it'd be nice to say we're going to do the same thing with all the zoo animals, but you have to be realistic. You can't go releasing just any zoo animal into the wild; it ain't gonna work. This was a studied, well-planned situation, one that took the coordinated efforts of dedicated people— all for a seriously endangered species. It would have been worth it even if it hadn't worked.

∧∧

In the spring of 1985, we had a birth that was the result of several years of work at the zoo: a white tiger cub was born to our two yellow tigers, Duke and Dolly. The cub was one of a litter of three, and had black stripes like the others, but white fur and blue eyes. Both parents carried the white and orange genes, so one out of four cubs may be white.

White tigers are very rare and valuable. There are fewer than one hundred in the world, and if a price tag had to be put on, it would be around $50,000. We wanted to have a nice attraction for Memorial Day weekend, provided the cub could stay healthy. But some white tigers have physical problems, and this one was no exception. She couldn't stand on her hind legs properly and risked becoming deformed if she stayed on the slick floor of the tiger den. She needed twenty-four-hour care in soft surroundings. At the time, there was no room in the zoo nursery for her.

By this time, our kids were all at school during the day, and Suzi hadn't raised an animal since our Knoxville days. I knew she was capable, so I asked her if she wanted to raise the white tiger cub at home. She accepted, and for six months, that tiger got special, around-the-clock tender loving care.

Suzi disinfected the kitchen floor every day on her hands and knees until the cub had her shots; she held her all the time and gave the cub her undivided attention. She even brought the cub to bed with her at night. I never got jealous, but I did move to the guest room. "I'm a light sleeper," I used to tell all the people who were ribbing me at the time. "I can't sleep with a woman and a tiger at the same time."

The cub grew up to be a magnificent specimen, thanks to Suzi's attention. For a long period after the tiger had been returned to the zoo, Suzi would go in and feed and care for it every night. It turned into a very special relationship, and still is to this day.

One early-summer evening, Suzi was exercising Taj—that

was her name—in an outside yard at the zoo. The tiger now weighed about a hundred pounds. Suzi came home just as it was getting dark. When she sat down on the couch, she felt her ring finger, turned bleach white and screamed.

"What's wrong?" I asked her. Suzi is always calm; I'd never seen her like this.

Taj and I when we were still friends—this was before she ate my wife's engagement ring. (Doug Martin)

"The diamond's gone out of my engagement ring," she said, and started crying. "Oh no . . . I must have lost it playing with Taj." There was a small scratch on her ring finger.

"Don't worry about it, Suzi," I told her. "We've got insurance. We'll get a diamond to put back in there." She'd had the ring for nineteen years, and I wasn't fazed by her losing that stone. I told her I loved her, to please stop crying, that it would be all right, but I couldn't console her.

The next day, she went back over to the zoo and cut the

Cleo the hippo gave birth right in the zoo yard, with thousands of encouraging fans cheering her on. This picture was taken within minutes of the birth (note the umbilical cord). (Columbus Zoo, Nancy Staley)

grass by hand for hours, looking for the stone. Her hands were blistered when she came back, and she was still very upset.

The same day, I got my maintenance crew together, and we went in the yard and mowed every blade of grass. I vacuumed it all up and stuck it in some big green plastic bags that I was going to take home to dump out and look through.

I left those bags outside the yard and went to my office for about an hour. In the meantime, the grounds crew came by, picked up the bags and fed that grass to the elephants. I called Suzi to tell her—big mistake—and now she fell apart all over again.

Suzi came back to the zoo, and we went over to the pachyderm yard, where the elephants had eaten about half the grass. Of course, now the job was going to be looking through elephant crap—I'd just gotten done looking through Taj's dung. For the next two days, we looked through elephant crap without finding anything. By then, this thing had turned into some kind of fiasco.

Of course, we never found the diamond, but the insurance company did pay the claim after a bit of a hassle. I hope nobody else's wife ever gets her diamond knocked out by a tiger, because that's probably one claim they'll only pay once. Suzi never got over it, even though we got her another diamond. Man, that was some bad scene. Paul Harvey liked the story so much, he used it on his newscast.

⋀⋀

Not all of our babies are delivered by the zoo stork. Some arrive mysteriously, the classic case of being left in a basket on the doorstep.

In the spring of 1986, Dan Badgley got an anonymous call to look for a Styrofoam container along the fence line by the parking lot. When he investigated, he was shocked to find two very young loggerhead sea turtles in the container.

A baby wolf playing possum. (Columbus Zoo, Julie Estadt)

Now, it's always exciting for a zoo to come into possession of rare animals, but loggerheads are an endangered species and possession requires a government permit. Our new arrivals were hot! We immediately notified the U.S. Fish and Wildlife Service and, after thinking it over, began an application to keep them.

Two months later, two more loggerheads were found in a bucket by the front gate (one of these did not survive). We don't know who left the turtles on our doorstep, but had that person been caught with them, he or she would have been subject to a fine of up to $5,000 and a possible six months in jail. Fooling with threatened animals is serious business.

What probably happened was that our "donor" was vacationing on a Florida beach and came upon a nest with hatchlings just emerging and heading for the sea. Probably innocently, the individual impulsively decided to bring a few home as "pets," only to find out later what they were and to learn the consequences of possessing them. That's where we came into the picture.

Once we got over the surprise of the donation, we had major decisions to make about their welfare. Sea turtles spend most of their lives at sea, going ashore only on the beach where they were hatched and then only to lay and bury their eggs before returning to sea.

This is a process that is poorly understood. Although we knew the home beach from a note left with the first two, we couldn't be assured of their welfare had we released them there because of the timing and other factors.

Once we decided to try to keep the turtles, the race was on. The survivors will reach their full adult size of about three hundred pounds by the age of five. But at the beginning, they were growing faster than we could build tanks for them. Ultimately, a group of contractors from the concrete industry came to our rescue with materials, and we constructed a nearly 10,000-gallon tank that should hold them through many healthy years.

Ika, the three-legged tiger. Ika killed his mate, Rewati, which is not terribly rare among big cats. (Columbus Dispatch)

ZOO
DEATHS

*S*ince only a tiny percentage of animals born in the zoo will ever go back to the wild, most will live out their lives in captivity. That's a fact of life, or death, if you will, and there's very little we can do about it. Around the zoo, we try to deal with it as practically as possible.

We lose a certain number of animals every month, and the public generally never hears about it. We can't go having burials and funerals for every zoo animal, the way kids do with their pet goldfish. Funerals are for human beings, not for animals.

But some zoo animals are more conspicuous by their absence than others. Some animals have been around for such a long time that their deaths touch both the public and the keepers who've been with them all this time; the news gets out that so-and-so passed away. There's nothing I can do about this or about how the people react. In some extreme cases, with my permission, an animal might even be buried on zoo grounds.

My critics in the zoo world will be disappointed to know that I'm basically against this. People are people and animals are animals. Besides, you don't bury a person at home. But if an animal dies who has somehow touched the entire community, I'll give the people and my staff whatever they feel is appropriate.

Hippopotamuses are old at twenty-five, but Pete, our oldest zoo resident, somehow made it to forty-four. Pete came to us from Egypt in 1939; he died in March 1982. This old guy was one of my personal favorites. He loved having water squirted in his mouth with a hose, and I always highlighted every zoo tour with a visit to his habitat. Pete was an institution.

Pete died on a Saturday night, which, in a sense, caught us by surprise. We knew he wasn't well, that his liver was in poor shape, but we hadn't planned on his leaving us so suddenly at such a time—by this, I mean four hours before the zoo opens for our busiest day. The public does not want to see a dead hippo, especially on a Sunday visit to the zoo.

When the keepers discovered sometime early Sunday morning that Pete had died, that didn't give us much time to remove his body from the pachyderm building.

When an animal of that size dies, people like to know, what do you do with the body? Well, we try to move as quickly as possible. You can't take a two-ton hippo and bring him out the door as deadweight; you have to cut him up—I know it sounds gruesome, but how else are we going to do it?

So we called Ohio State's veterinary department and had the veterinary students come over to help transport Pete on a truck, piece by piece. They had to use chain saws and it was literally a mess.

In addition—and this is important—a necropsy had to be performed, and we didn't want to hurry this unnecessarily. Some of the keepers had been with this animal twenty years. I told them they didn't have to assist with this if they didn't want to. They said no, the animal was dead, and they wanted to learn more about hippos. It's not every day of the week that a necropsy is done on a hippo, and this was an opportunity to learn more.

We found out that Pete died from a massively enlarged liver. That and other vital organs were given to the animal labs at OSU for further study, and the rest of Pete went into the incinerator.

We weren't the only ones who missed Pete. Cleo, his longtime companion, knew something was wrong, too. She was off her feed for months after his death.

But there's a nice postscript to Pete's death. Cleo was so sad we decided to get her another companion. We got Big Bake, a ten-month-old hippo from the Houston Zoo, about six months later. Big Bake was named after Glenn Baker, our maintenance foreman, who drove the 650-pound pachyderm straight through from Texas in a converted horse trailer.

The trip took twenty-eight hours and included ten stops at service stations along the way while Baker and his crew watered down the hippo to make sure his skin stayed moist. Gas station attendants, who got a big kick out of this, were very helpful, and Big Bake arrived in fine shape. When he got here, he took a big, long drink of water and relaxed right into his new home next to Cleo. In fact, they produced a youngster much earlier than we expected.

〰〰

Things can always suddenly go very wrong when you're breeding wild animals in captivity. You just never know. You hope for the best, knowing that it's risky business and that the rewards can be very great.

Rewati was a beautiful twelve-year-old female white tiger on loan to us from the National Zoo in Washington, D.C. Her mother had been a gift to the United States from the people of India, and Rewati was the first white tiger born in this country. Dr. Ted Reed, the former director at the National Zoo and one of the most renowned leaders in the zoo world, had raised Rewati in his home. It was through Dr. Reed's sister, who lived here in Columbus, that we were able to acquire Rewati for breeding.

Ika was a four-hundred-pound, three-legged former circus tiger who had lost his leg to an infection before coming to our zoo. Over a period of nine months, Ika began his courtship of Rewati in an adjacent pen. When the time was right, we introduced them, and for the first two weeks, it seemed like a marriage made in heaven. They got along fine.

One evening during their third week together, I was playing tennis with Suzi when I saw head curator Mike July come walking toward me down the hill next to the courts. Oh no, I thought, what now?

"Jack, Jack," he yelled. "Come here, quick."

"What is it, Mike?" I yelled back at him. "What's wrong?"

"Ika just killed Rewati," he shouted, loud enough for players on courts next to us to hear. It was about 7 P.M., the sun going down—a beautiful, peaceful summer evening. Everybody stopped playing.

"What?" I walked over to the fence.

"Ika just killed Rewati—broke her neck."

"I don't believe it," I said. "They've been getting along fine."

"Well, apparently they were mating," explained Mike, "and he just snapped her neck. It's known to happen."

I still couldn't believe it. I dropped my racket and rushed over to the zoo. When I got there, they were just hauling her away. There were two small sets of puncture wounds on the skin, but her neck had been severely snapped. The strangest part of the scene was Ika, who just lay there in the corner purring, like nothing had ever happened. I felt terrible, and now I had to call Dr. Reed.

Fortunately, Dr. Reed understood the situation—in fact, much better than I did. I told him exactly what happened and apologized. He told me those things happen, not to worry about it, and to send him an autopsy report, which I did.

I still felt indirectly responsible, in that we put two animals together that wouldn't necessarily have selected each other in the wild. Was there some way we could have known this might happen? They did get along great during those two weeks—then all of a sudden the male goes and cracks the female's neck. And how could a three-legged tiger kill a four-legged tiger anyway? Since then, Ika has successfully bred and produced several litters of cubs. In fact, he sired Taj's first litter in 1988, which resulted in two white cubs being born.

∧∧

Like most of us, I hate funerals. I never attend them; the next funeral I go to will be my own and that's it. So I wasn't exactly thrilled when the gorilla keepers asked if they could pay their respects by having a small funeral for Mac the gorilla on the zoo grounds.

Mac (Macombo) was the clan patriarch when he died of a heart attack at age thirty-eight in June 1984. He was also a granddaddy, an important one, having sired the first gorilla born in captivity. He'd been wild-caught and brought to Columbus in 1951. The keepers all loved him, and he was probably the most fondly regarded animal in the whole zoo.

Dianna Frisch called me to say that she'd found Mac dead when she came in that morning. She said it appeared that Mac had died quite suddenly, without suffering. I was saddened, because I loved Mac and also because he represented both the old and the new zoo. He had been caught in Africa and lived in a cage most of his life.

It was after Mac's body had been transferred over to Ohio State for necropsy that the keepers asked me if we could bring him back for a zoo burial.

I said I'd have to check with the trustees, and we'd see. After thinking about it, I realized it would be a nice thing to do something for all the people who wanted to remember Mac, but the last thing I wanted was for people to see this as a PR gimmick.

So we got the green light and went ahead with the memorial. At first, it was just going to be a quiet affair with keepers, a "members of the immediate family" type of thing, but then it began to grow. Docents, volunteers who had worked with Mac over the past twenty years, started calling and asking to come, the papers announced the "funeral" and some public showed up. I guess it was unavoidable.

I wanted the keepers to take care of it, but they asked me to say something at the ceremony. Say something? What was I going to say about a gorilla? You'll think of something, they told me, you always do.

On a beautiful weekday morning, there were about three hundred people gathered outside the gates, waiting for the ceremony. The maintenance people had built a beautiful casket with "Mac" inscribed in rope on the top. They picked him up in a zoo truck, and it took eight sturdy pallbearers to lift it with him in there.

At the appointed time, I could hardly get near the grave site, which we had decided would be next to the gorilla

Animals are never buried on zoo grounds, but since Mac spent thirty-four years in our zoo, fathered the first gorilla born in captivity, and became the zoo's senior patriarch, we made an exception. (Columbus Citizen Journal, Tom Wilcox)

habitat. There were people crowded all around and piles and piles of flowers everywhere. I remember thinking this was kind of bizarre. This could be the funeral of a really important person.

Usually, I'm never stuck for words, but here I was at a gorilla funeral, and I was stuck. Other people spoke first— it was informal and very touching, very respectful. Dianna Frisch said something about how Mac could be a colossal pain in the butt to all who knew him, and how you either loved him or you hated him, but you always respected him.

Then I got up there and said, "We're all here today to pay respects to the first gorilla to breed successfully in captivity; Mac's contribution to the survival of the species will live on, long after we're all gone. Animals are usually not buried on zoo grounds, but we felt Mac and the community deserved it, because of what he had done not only for the zoo but for the gorilla species. We've learned a great deal from Mac, and that's why we're here, and that's why he'll be buried here where he spent nearly all his life."

The gorillas were outdoors, and Mac's two youngsters, Oscar and Toni, were looking on. It was real quiet, and people said later the apes knew what was going on. I don't believe that, but I know they were watching the crowd, and I know that with its being so quiet they knew something was up.

"Ashes to ashes, dust to dust; Mac did a great job for all of us," was how I closed it up. I let the flowers stay for a few days, and then we took everything away. Today, there's a plaque at the site.

Predictably, I took some criticism from one individual in the zoo world whose ideas are usually diametrically opposed to mine. But you can't please everybody, and most of the time, you have to take care of your own. I think Mac got a nice send-off.

My daughter Kathaleen co-hosted Hanna's Ark, *my first TV show.* (Sea World of Ohio)

14

"HEEEERE'S JACK!"

All this television stuff started, unintentionally, when I got to Columbus. After seeing me in some colorful local news interviews, the producer of a cable talk show asked me if I'd do some animal episodes. As an opportunity to promote the zoo, I accepted, even if it wasn't exactly prime time. But it wouldn't have mattered to me if it were high school radio, I'd have done it then, and I still would today.

My next stop on the local circuit was *Hanna's Ark*, a family-type show on WBNS (CBS) that featured my daughter Kathaleen and me as co-hosts (though only eleven, she stole the show every time). We would open with an animal at the zoo, then go to footage of the same species in the wild, then come back and close from the zoo. I loved the concept, and it was fun while it lasted.

After two years and forty-eight eipsodes, *Hanna's Ark* was shelved. I was somewhat upset at the time, since the station announced that because we had a small zoo, we didn't have enough animals to tie in to the wild. Tell the people that *Hee Haw* was creeping up on us—which it was—but don't tell me, a zoo director with some 6,000 animals, that we don't have enough animals left.

But ending *Hanna's Ark* was a mixed blessing. Shortly afterward, Channel 4, the local NBC affiliate, offered me a

series of one-hour wildlife specials. These shows have enabled me to learn (as I teach) about wild animals at the
farthest reaches of the earth (to date, we've done Egypt,
East Africa, China, India, the Galápagos and Alaska) and
have resulted in an avalanche of invaluable publicity for the
zoo.

A special bonus to our agreement is a small weekly bit
that I do every Friday on their noon news called Zoo Day.
I take an animal to the studio, or a crew comes to us, and
we just talk about what's going on at the zoo. Talk about
priceless promotion; this is a fantastic weekend reminder,
especially in light of the fact that zoo attendance is usually
based on the impulse visit—the guy who says to his wife,
"Hey, I know what, honey—let's take the kids to the zoo." .

Angela Pace, the anchorperson for my first five years of
Zoo Days, was, at the beginning, deadly opposed to the
segment—she thought it had no place on a serious newscast. But we hit it off so well and had so many good times
together that it didn't take long for her to come around.

Our greatest Zoo Day segment ever was the one on
which Betty White, my favorite camel, urinated all over the
floor—on the air, of course. Betty White didn't just urinate,
however; she let out what sounded like a torrential down-
pour splashing down on the studio floor—something like
when you've got a busted roof gutter in a thunderstorm. It
was way too loud to ignore, so I just interrupted my spiel
on what the camel ate, where it was from, etc., and said,
"Oh, look, Angela, Betty's going to the bathroom."

Angela, meanwhile, was trying to step out of the camel's
way. I figured we'd better get Betty off, so I went to pull
her with the rope, but she slipped in her own urine and
ended up knocking me and Angela down. Next, I brought
out a few little goats, since it was Good Friday and I wanted
to promote spring fever at our Children's Zoo. I guess they
must have all just eaten, because when they got to the same
spot, they all started going to the bathroom, too. By now,
I was laughing so hard I was crying; Angela was trying hard
to maintain her composure.

"Let's have one more look at Betty White," I said to Angela.

"No, uh . . . Jack, I don't think we have time," said Angela, just as Betty came storming back in, butting Angela out of her way and onto the floor again. In one split second, she was in and out of the frame.

As Angela picked herself up off the floor to sign off, I went to grab Betty White, who was now standing in a corner of the studio. In traditional camel fashion, she wouldn't budge. The last thing the viewer saw was me tugging on that camel, with the picture jumping up and down from the camerman laughing so hard.

⋀⋀

My big start on national television came in 1983 from ABC's *Good Morning America*. Associate producer Patty Neger had seen on the AP wire service a story about the twin gorillas being born here in Columbus and called me. She asked if they could do a live remote with me from the zoo, and I said fine. It all went off very smoothly, but I have to say it's hard to miss with a couple of twin baby gorillas.

A year later Patty checked in on us again with the idea of doing a birthday party for the twins. We had a birthday cake, the whole bit, and by this time the twins were total hams. They were all over me, pulling my earphone out and chewing my safari shirt. The *GMA* people liked it, and Patty told me to call her if there were any more significant births happening at the zoo.

The following spring, while in New York on some other business, I told Patty about Taj, the white tiger cub born to

*P*atty Neger (here with her friend Gertie) gave me my start on national television when she featured our twin gorillas on *Good Morning America*. (Suzi Hanna)

yellow parents that Suzi was raising at home, because of the cub's leg disability. Patty said they had a last-minute opening, could I get Taj to New York immediately? Suzi wasn't home, but the *GMA* people somehow managed to track her down on the golf course during Jack Nicklaus' Memorial Tournament. Hours later, Taj was on her way to New York City, and the next morning, she joined me for my first *Good Morning America* studio appearance with Joan Lunden. She "aawwwed" 'em.

My next appearance was again in the studio, with two lion cubs and a sandhill crane. Kathleen Sullivan was the host and that crane was flapping its huge wings so much that Kathleen's hair was blowing like she was in a wind tunnel. The cubs were crawling all over my lap, and I just went on with the interview as though nothing was happening.

What I was going through was nothing compared to Debbie Casto's ordeal the night before. Debbie, our marketing director, had just been kicked out of the Plaza Athénée Hotel. Around ten o'clock, she had taken one of the lion cubs for a walk on the marble floor of the hotel's foyer, and somebody got uptight. Debbie wound up sleeping in the manager's office on a cot with the two cubs.

Anyway, that particular show cemented *Good Morning America*'s relationship with the Columbus Zoo. Producer Sonya Selby-Wright suggested having me appear on a monthly basis, and at the same time *GMA* officially "adopted" the Columbus Zoo with the twins' second birthday party. An aardvark and a couple of baby wallabies (kangaroos) were presented on the air to hosts David Hartman and Joan Lunden, with the understanding that *GMA* would adopt them, which includes the cost of feeding the animals for a year.

For the first segment under the new arrangement, Joan Lunden traveled out to the zoo. We greeted her at the front gate with a welcoming committee that looked like a Noah's Ark with zookeepers. Joan Lunden loves animals, and aside

After Good Morning America "adopted" the zoo, Joan Lunden, a genuine animal lover, invited us to film a live remote segment. Here we are in the zoo kitchen, where over $250,000 worth of food is dispensed yearly. (Columbus Zoo, Rick Prebeg)

from an embarrassing moment when Oscar the gorilla disrespectfully nailed her with a crap toss, she had a great time touring the zoo.

It makes it much easier for everyone when a TV personality likes the animals that I bring on, especially on live television. There are no rehearsals, so it's hard to predict a tense situation, and, of course, it's a well-known fact that animals react differently to tension in human beings.

Once, I brought a big python on *GMA;* I think I was doing a show about animals that don't make good pets. Like me, Joan Lunden was a bona fide animal lover—as a kid, she even wanted to be like Marlin Perkins—so I figured any animal was fine on the set. I didn't know she was afraid of snakes.

The snake wasn't aggressive or anything, and I didn't taunt her with it, like I might do jokingly with David

Letterman. But I realized, just after I'd pulled it out of its box, that something was seriously wrong. Joan became pale, and I could see the fear in her eyes. She just said no, no, and I knew she wasn't kidding. People can faint, even the most professional of TV hosts, before a nationwide live audience. So I backed off and came up with a parrot while she regained her composure. Now, it's not like she fell apart or anything—it was just a potentially bad scene. She jokes about it today.

Every time I travel to New York for Good Morning America, a whole menagerie of animals and keepers accompanies me. Charlie Gibson, who was bitten by a fox in one segment, here eyes my donkey warily. (© 1988 Capital Cities/ABC, Inc.)

Charlie Gibson, who took over as co-host from David Hartman, also had a nasty moment, just before we went on. It was Charlie's first week, it was a brand-new set and it was my first appearance with him. There was a large group of television reporters on the set, and I'd brought along a cougar, a red-tailed hawk and a fox for my talk about North American predators.

About thirty seconds before our cue to go on, I took the fox out of the cage, and it tried to nip me a little, nothing too bad. I held it firmly in my lap, and as Charlie sat down opposite me, he asked to hold the fox. I couldn't say no—actually, I could have and should have, but I didn't. I handed Charlie the fox, and it bit him hard on the index finger.

With only a few seconds until we were on, Charlie let the fox down without saying a word and reached into his pocket for a handkerchief to smother his bleeding finger. "Today, we have Jack Hanna with us from the Columbus Zoo," he said, on cue, without any reference to the bite.

Meanwhile, I was holding a cougar, and the fox was running all over the set. Charlie asked me some questions very professionally, while I tried hard not to look at his finger, which was bleeding like a stuck pig.

The minute the show was over, Charlie just asked me what kind of shots he needed, before rushing off to a doctor. I told him tetanus shots, but I didn't tell him foxes can carry rabies. A photographer from the New York *Post* was there, and Charlie got a lot of mileage from the bite in the next day's paper. I was on *Late Night* the following week, and, predictably, Letterman had a few laughs at Charlie's and my expense.

The agreement that we have with *Good Morning America* is a prime example of how the public is changing in its perception of zoos. We're more concerned with preserving species than we are with showing off exotic animals. The image *GMA* was trying to project with the zoo segments was one where the viewer would learn something (often about threatened or endangered species) and still enjoy the animal as well. (For Letterman, you can just turn that around.)

Most people don't know that I don't earn big bucks from all the television shows I do, including Letterman and *GMA*. I'm representing the Columbus Zoo, and as such, I don't expect to become a millionaire. The expenses—which, with animal travel, can be considerable—are all covered by the networks, and no taxpayer dollars are ever involved. But the amount of TV time that we accumulate in a year would come to hundreds of thousands of dollars if we had to buy it in advertising. It's a trade-off and a huge bonus for us.

Ask people on the street what the number one zoo in the country is, and most of them will tell you the San Diego Zoo; ask the same people if they've ever been there, and 95 percent will probably say no. How come it's ranked as one of the top zoos in the United States? Because of media exposure, marketing and PR; they've done a great job at it. Also, it doesn't hurt that San Diego happens to be one of the finest zoos in the world. But the point is, Joan Embery has done a fabulous job marketing the San Diego Zoo with her appearances on Johnny Carson and other shows over the years.

Now, what I do on the David Letterman show is different; it's not the same audience as the Carson show, nor have I ever tried to be like Joan Embery. My philosophy is to entertain and hope people learn, rather than to teach and hope people are entertained. I'm a character on David Letterman, and I accept that role—it's not all that much different from me in real life anyway, especially when I'm away from the zoo. It's also very different from what I do for *Good Morning America*. People play for laughs on Letterman, which is something we've managed to do for four years now without demeaning or hurting any of the animals, regardless of what my critics may say—a few of them say plenty.

But despite the laughs, people do learn about animals on the Letterman shows, too. I'd like to think that even David Letterman, between all the jokes and the put-downs, has managed to learn something about animals, not necessarily from me but from the animals themselves. They're the real stars.

∧∧

I'd been doing *Good Morning America* for about a year when I received a call from Laurie Lennard, the talent coordinator for NBC's *Late Night with David Letterman.* They were looking for an animal person who could get along with Dave, and Patty Neger had referred me, saying I was just the guy.

Well, I hated to admit it, but I had never watched the show, mainly because of my job hours. I'd heard of it, but never seen it—it comes on when I'm in bed. All the same, I said sure, I'd go on, just tell me when.

Meanwhile, the local media all came to me saying, "Don't go on that show, he'll tear you apart," and other things like that. I thought he was just a talk-show host like Carson, and I wondered what they were talking about. Tear me up? What's he want to tear me up for? I'm just a nobody—he isn't going to tear me up. No way I was turning down this show. I guess my curiosity got to me.

On Valentine's Day 1985, my first *Late Night* date, snow threatened to cancel the whole thing. We were going to take the animals east in a zoo van, but the roads were mostly closed and travel was impossible, especially with exotic animals. I was desperate, but I knew we'd get there somehow. If I called the Letterman people and said I couldn't make it, what were my chances of ever being asked back?

A friend of mine, Dale Eisenman, said he'd fly all the animals, no problem. Most of the animals were small, but I decided not to tell him about Spinner, the eighty-five-pound baby pygmy hippo. The animals wouldn't fit in his plane, so he found another one and pulled the back seats out so that Spinner, two capuchin monkeys, a pelican, a crow, a European hedgehog and a pig could all squeeze in. The cockroaches went with me on a commercial flight, in my left-hand pocket, like always.

People are always asking me, what is this thing I have

with cockroaches? Well, they're quiet, they don't smell, they eat leftovers and, if I bring them out at the right moment, they're show-stoppers. They're my buddies. They go everywhere with me. My calling card even has a cockroach on it.

The animals got to the NBC studios in Rockefeller Center just in time for the show, and I was totally psyched, pumped up and ready to show our zoo to the entire country. Some people think I'm nervous before shows, and I sometimes am, but I don't want to be calmed down. This is the way I operate. The animals will calm me down. In this particular case, I was apprehensive not knowing what to expect from David Letterman.

David and I met on the air, the way it is with most of his guests. I brought the capuchin monkeys out, and got a big laugh when I told him they didn't like women. I caught some flak for this, but, hey, it's a fact—they don't like women. The pelican wouldn't eat the fish, Henry the crow flew up into the audience and wouldn't come back, the cockroaches got away from me on David's desk and the pig was running around all over the place. We—my staff and I—just kind of let things happen. David was very polite and courteous, and I knew he liked the pygmy hippo. But I do remember him looking at me like I might be a little crazy.

That first show went off beautifully, and although I didn't plan it or realize it then, the helter-skelter, animals-all-over-the-place idea set the trend for future appearances. That's called finding your niche. People who know me know I'm at my best when I'm doing fifty things at once. I just wished that crow had come back like he was supposed to—it took five hours after the show was over to get him back so we could leave Rockefeller Center for Columbus.

The producers were pleased and even asked me not to plan any other late-night talk-show appearances. I took this as a good sign. I knew the host had had a good time, and I knew this was important in terms of being invited back. When they officially asked me, a month later, if I could appear during ratings week in May, I was elated.

For the next show, I brought up two young elephants, Boomer and Belle, who weighed in at two thousand pounds each. They barely fit in the freight elevators in Rockefeller Center; another six months and I would have been out of luck.

The pachyderms were a big hit, and it was on this show that David started to kid me a bit. He asked me how the lesser anteater I'd brought on the show got his name, and I said, "Because they eat less ants than other anteaters." He made a face, like sure, Jack, and everybody laughed. I wasn't trying to be funny or to set myself up; I was just kind of preoccupied when he asked—some animal had disappeared under his desk. It wouldn't be long before he'd be telling me that I wasn't really a zoo director, that there really wasn't any zoo in Columbus.

Everything on the Letterman show happens spontaneously; there is no script. Producer Robert Morton says all the time that no one ever knows what's going to happen when I come on, which I guess is mostly true. But we still have to have the animal situation under control—you can't just bring them out in any order.

Once we had a cheetah for the show, with a variety of other animals, half of which might be the cheetah's prey in the wild. As I was going over the list with Morty beforehand, he asked me, where was our "payoff animal"? We were starting with the cheetah and ending with a Chinese pheasant, and I think he would have liked it the other way around. "Morty," I told him, "we can't bring the cheetah on with those other animals—we'd have a bloodbath."

We bring animals on the basis of their availability, their health (they're all checked by keepers and veterinarians before they travel), their temperament—how they'll react to rock music, for example—and we also try to vary the selection from show to show. Ideally, I'd like to have as many "payoff" animals as possible on there. They're all "payoff" animals as far as I'm concerned, but I know that if I bring on a snail and a housecat, my future on the show wouldn't be too bright.

In a sense, I'm between a rock and a hard place on this. The producers would like to have wild animals running all over the place—that's the big payoff. But just as a singer knows what songs he can sing and in what style, as a zoo director, I know what animals I can handle, where I can put them, how fast I can pick one up and a host of other intangibles that crop up. Dave obviously has to get the laughs, that's what the show's for, but I'm also out there to make sure nobody gets hurt; him, me or the animals. I'm also concerned that the viewing audience might learn a little something about the animal as well.

Aardvarks, as everyone knows, eat ants... (Columbus Dispatch)

One of our nuttiest visits ever was when I brought up a couple of full-grown camels. I weighed and measured them, like I do with all the animals before we come on, but I forgot to measure their humps. They had plenty of room in the elevator, but the ceiling where they got off was too low. (I realized all this after it was too late.) We walked them down the hallway to the studio and they took out just about every ceiling panel—ruined them, lights, everything. Their humps just popped everything out. Once a camel's walking straight in a narrow hallway, you can hardly turn him around. It was a mess.

... But David Letterman wasn't quite sure whether to believe it or not. (Columbus Dispatch)

The building manager came up and really let me have it. I apologized and told him I'd pay for the damage. He told me this would cost more than $5,000. By now, a crowd of NBC personnel had gathered around like it was a big party—we probably cleared every office on the entire floor. I'd been trying to concentrate on the show coming up and now I was a wreck about the damage.

Barry Sands, who was *Late Night*'s producer then, came out and told me not to worry about it, that the building people don't run the show. I told Barry I was really sorry, but I never noticed that he had a camera shooting this whole fiasco, that he was going to open the show with it. It looked like a tornado had struck.

Well, of course, all this was a big hit. David just shook his head at me and said, "Oh, Jack, Jack . . . ," like can't you ever just come up here and be normal? If I ever did, we probably wouldn't be asked back too often. We had a tense moment when David got on the camel and almost hit his head on one of the studio spotlights, but otherwise the show went great.

The maintenance people had fixed a few panels and three or four lights before it was time for us to leave. This wasn't too smart, since we had to get the camels back downstairs again. Our dromedaries knocked those same lights and panels out and now the building guy was doubly mad. Ever since then, they put us in a maintenance room; we no longer get a dressing room. But that's fine with us; we don't care what we have as long as we can mop up all the mess.

Another wild Letterman experience was when I got bitten on camera. I took on a young twenty-pound beaver that I hadn't handled previously. All went well while I held her on my lap, and I then demonstrated how she could swim by placing her in a glass tank in front of Dave's desk.

She was still okay as I lifted her from the tank—with dripping water drenching me and the stage floor. As I got up to take the beaver off during the commercial break, she started to slide out of my hands. I grasped the base of her tail with my right hand, and she chomped down on the space between my left thumb and index finger; I slid on the wet floor, went down on one knee, scrambled up and hung on to the beaver until an assistant repossessed her. And all this on camera. Not one of my more graceful exits.

In the two minutes allotted to the commercial break, I wrapped paper towels around my bleeding hand and slipped on a flesh-colored rubber glove just as we went back on the air. Sometimes the show must go on. We finished the segment, which included electric eels, a Chinese crested dog and a yak. The glove on my left hand was rapidly filling with blood, so I was very anxious for the segment to end—especially before Dave had a chance to make some comment about my beaver bite. After a brief visit to Roosevelt

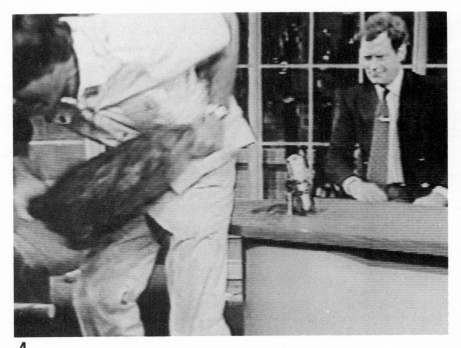

A beaver bite in midair, as America looks on. (Columbus Zoo, Rick Prebeg, off monitor of Letterman tape)

*S*pinner the pygmy hippo before the Letterman show.
(Columbus Citizen Journal, Tom Wilcox)

Hospital in Manhattan, I was on my way home for my weekly news show. And guess what animal I was to bring along. Bucky Beaver! She didn't bite me, but then again I never want to touch or look at another beaver as long as I live—male *or* female!

If you keep in mind that the beaver's front teeth are built for sawing logs, you know that my hand got it pretty good. I had no feeling in my thumb for a while . . . and a red face for even longer.

So at some point I became the straight man and started bearing the brunt of David Letterman's jokes. I don't mind, I really don't. I receive a dozen or so letters after every appearance from people who feel bad about him putting me down. But I know David loves animals, he treats them better than he does most of his guests. And I'm always amazed at his knack for coming up with the lines:

"Have these guys been eating onions, Jack?"—when I brought out the twin gorillas.

"Is this your idea of a good time in Columbus?"—when I showed him how a chinchilla takes a dust bath.

"Now, this is a female, right?"—when I had him milk a goat.

Of course, sometimes I step into it. Like when he's asking me how far a particular bird will fly, and I'll say, "Oh, they'll fly real far, Dave." He'll just sit and look at me without saying anything for a few seconds, the audience will laugh, and I'll think, uh-oh . . . here it comes. "You're not a zoo director, are you, Jack?" he'll say. "There is no zoo in Columbus, is there?"

I'm asked all the time if I think David Letterman will ever visit the Columbus Zoo. I don't know. I guess the reason I've never really invited him is that I don't want him to look at me and say, "Are you kidding me? Jack, I would rather watch a log float into the Hudson than come out to your zoo."

∧∧

Without my keeper staff and zoo assistants, there would be no *Good Morning America* or David Letterman shows for

Jack Hanna, no television shows of any kind, for that matter. In fact, I probably couldn't give a speech at a grade school without somebody to help me with the animals.

The job for Betty Leitzen, Suzi Rapp, Jennie Pettit or any of the other people who help transport the animals begins days prior to a scheduled appearance. They go over all the animals before leaving, then they spend long hours on the road or in the air getting them to their destination. These people are all trained and experienced with this; they live, eat and sleep with those animals. Once they arrive, we have a meeting based on what they've observed—the animals' conditions in transit, maybe a change in temperament, whatever.

During each show, I have three or four keepers stationed off-camera, ready to correct any situation that might arise. They know when or when not to come on, when to keep an animal from going into the audience. They're a very dedicated group of people.

Betty and her colleagues have a particularly tough time when it comes to motels and hotels. They're always looking for a place for the night. Most places don't allow pets, much less zoo animals. It's tough enough just to sneak the animals in, but most of them have to be exercised, cleaned, watered and fed. But Betty and the crew somehow always manage.

If she's given a second-floor room at a motel, she'll say she's afraid of fire, so that they can get a first-floor room where the animals can be whisked in and out. Betty's learned to be brazen and fast; just back the van right up to the room and move 'em in.

If a young lion starts to growl, she'll turn the TV up loud. Better they call and ask you to turn the TV down than find out you have a lion cub and ask you to leave in the middle of the night. If you're caught the next morning, you just show that the room's clean, give them some zoo T-shirts and say thank you and goodbye.

We're very fortunate in this respect to have discovered New York City's Mayflower Hotel on Central Park West.

You can take your pets there; we know—we've had everything from gorillas to alligators to lions up there. And you know what? Those nice people actually don't mind.

The hotel's owners, Mr. and Mrs. Avalon, are animal lovers and they have but one request: that they and their son Reynolds be allowed to come up and spend some time with our crew and the animals. Of course, Betty and the staff are only too happy to indulge them, unless they're busy exercising a tiger in the hallway or maybe walking some goats in the park.

One of the toughest things is the constant lack of sleep. Many of the animals are nocturnal; an owl will hoot, a cat will pace, an alligator in the bathtub will thrash and splash around all night. After three or four days of this, you can turn into a zombie. But I've never heard anyone complain, and the animals seem to enjoy their short vacation from the zoo.

In the fall of 1988, I decided to give Betty and her assistants a break from traveling to New York by zoo van. It may have been a break for Betty, but the pilot of a small private plane I chartered didn't see it that way. We were scheduled for a *Good Morning America* appearance and the animals had to be transported to New York with only a few hours' notice. The pilot was told that only one small monkey would be with a keeper on the flight. However, twenty minutes before the plane took off, Betty arrived at the airport with two baby orangutans, a twenty-five-pound sea turtle inside a hundred-gallon fish tank filled with water, a three-foot alligator, a fourteen-week-old Bengal tiger and a serval cat from Africa, along with three keepers. It's amazing, but they all fit on that small plane, and of course the pilot will have a story to tell for years to come.

The keepers feel fortunate to go on national TV; they also get to travel, and they get to participate in whatever public relations we might have. They receive credit for their hard work back at the zoo that they might not ordinarily receive if the Columbus Zoo weren't in the spotlight. I try

*M*eeting Marlin Perkins, my childhood hero, was a great thrill for me. Without his efforts on Wild Kingdom, *animals would have much less visibility today—on television and elsewhere.* (Jack Hanna)

to give everyone the opportunity to participate, and I'm grateful that they do so with so much enthusiasm. I could never do it without them.

The Columbus Zoo animals have appeared on many television shows across the country and not once has a host, an animal or the viewing audience been harmed (with the exception of Charlie Gibson). I would also like to add that 95 percent of these animals are currently reproducing and raising families of their own after returning to their own zoo, which, after all, is what zoos are all about!

A safari group in East Africa with Suzi and me. (Georgiann Kindler)

15

ON
SAFARI

One of the great assets of being a zoo director is the occasional trip to the wild, a chance to see the animals in their natural habitats. I have my job to thank for all my unique travels abroad, but most especially for the glorious experience of travels in the Dark Continent.

All of my safaris to Africa have been with groups from Columbus that I've helped organize. It doesn't make the experience any less sensational, just a little more exhausting. You want the people to have a good time, which they can't have if their luggage or passports are lost. I have to make sure interpreters understand what people need. If somebody has diarrhea, I've got to make sure their van stops at a bathroom, not a tourist shop where they can get more film. I've seen a guy go in his pants in the jeep.

Somebody's tent may be overlooking a plain where zebra graze, but they'd rather overlook the area where the elephants are watering. Somebody would like California chardonnay rather than South African white wine. Somebody moves around too much while somebody else is trying to take pictures—I've got to be a master social director just to figure out the van arrangements.

Now, after eight trips to Africa, I have a few meetings before we go to try to straighten things out as much as possible. If I get a question like "What kind of air condition-ing will we have over there?" or "What's the insurance situation over there?" well, I'll do my best to discourage these people from going. I'd love to see somebody try to sue in Africa—who do you sue, the animal?

Travelers worry too much about clothes. We're not going macheteing through the jungle in search of King Kong. Sneakers are fine—you don't need boots that go up to your knees. People go out and spend several hundred dollars at Banana Republic buying everything from pith helmets to safari shirts. The locals in Nairobi always get a big laugh seeing each new load of tourists in their brand-new safari threads.

Now, when they come back after a couple of weeks, they look like they've been on safari. Some have beards, some may have dropped five pounds. They understand what it is to have a scotch and water without ice, or—and this is a big gripe—to have a beer that's not ice cold. I guess that falls under "roughing it."

⋀⋀

Kenya is safari paradise. It's the best place to start for any first-time visitor, despite any minor discomforts or incon-veniences. Plus it's an easy place to get to, and if you find a good tour outfit, it's a sure way to know that your people will sleep and eat well and will be protected.

The vehicles and drivers are always important. The vans—we have Range Rovers—take an incredible amount of punishment, sometimes in places where there are no roads. The drivers must be good mechanics. If I took a group to Nairobi and picked out tents and vehicles on my own, we'd probably get as far as the suburbs. And the food—some-times they get these fantastic meals out to people six, seven hours away in the middle of nowhere, you're amazed how they do it.

If you want a little rougher safari, you can go to other countries, perhaps take a camping trip by truck in Tanzania or hike and camp up in Rwanda—that might be a next step

On safari in India, looking for Bengal tigers. (Columbus Zoo file)

for some. But the best place to experience Africa the first time is Kenya.

The first game run is always a great thrill for me, not just to see the animals again—and by the way, there is always something different to see in Africa, always—but to see the reactions of people seeing their first animals in the wild. It might be a mother elephant munching on a bush with her baby walking alongside, or three or four giraffes crossing the road, or a pride of lions sleeping in the grass. Everyone is in total wonderment.

A few years back, we were out on the Masai Mara Game Reserve on the Serengeti Plain on our very first day when we came across two lions mating. They totally ignored us, which is understandable, since they'll copulate up to twenty times a day when the lioness is in heat. A little while later, we scored again, witnessing a lion kill, which is always fascinating, as well as very rare, to see. After the cat was finished eating, hyenas came in packs for the bones, followed by jackals, while vultures circled overhead. There is no waste in Africa.

Another fascinating observation on the Serengeti is how a herd of wildebeest or antelopes will graze hardly two hundred yards from a pride of lions. The wildebeest know when the lions aren't hungry; they'll also know when the hunt begins.

But among safari people, the ultimate in big-game watching is to see the "big five": lion, rhinoceros, elephant, Cape buffalo and leopard or cheetah. Of course, this is a bit of hype from tour guides, because, after all, there's so much to see from aardvarks to zebras, from warthogs to hippos. But it's considered a big deal to see the "big five."

In the camp at night, people sit around the campfire comparing animals they've seen. It's the funniest thing; they'll all be trying to outdo each other. In a way, I am sure

A herd of wildebeest crossing the Serengeti Plain. (Robert Mauck)

it was like the big-game hunters who argued over who bagged the biggest elephant or who shot the largest buffalo.

"Wow! We saw a giraffe, an elephant and a leopard within two hundred feet of each other."

"Oh yeah? We saw two or three giraffes, a whole herd of elephants and a leopard, all in one area."

"Well, our driver, Peter, took us to a pool where there must have been twenty-five or thirty hippos."

"Really? We didn't see any hippos."

Now I'll have a problem with the people in James's van; nobody wants to go with him the next day. They all want to go with Peter, because James didn't find any hippos, even if it wasn't his fault.

Then there's always, always the camera equipment. Boy, you'd think everybody was working for *National Geographic*.

"I got a picture of elephants mating."

"I got a picture of lions mating."

"Yeah, well that's 'cause you have a two-hundred-millimeter lens and all I've got is a fifty-millimeter."

And the professional gear that some of these people bring along is absolutely phenomenal—tripods and huge, heavy lenses; I don't know how they manage to lug it all around. They all laugh at me, because once I brought along one of those little yellow underwater cameras—you know, the kind they used to advertise would work in your bathtub. Everybody thought I was nuts.

Suzi takes all the pictures in our family. I must admit that I have never taken one picture on any safari anyplace in the world, never clicked one camera—unless it was for a person who wanted a shot of himself and his wife in front of Mount Kilimanjaro. I just don't have the patience, and besides, I've got all the pictures inside my head.

∧∧

Nighttime on the Serengeti is something else. There's a very romantic, exotic feeling in the air, and with the stars, the campfire and all the animal sounds, it's just like in the movies.

I'll never forget my first night in camp. I heard hyenas

screaming, zebras doing their call and lions roaring. The sound of a lion roaring in the middle of the night will send a chill up your spine. I could not sleep a wink that first night. I kept waiting for a snake or a deadly insect to crawl into my tent. But that's the least of your worries; the only snake I've seen in all my trips was a Gaboon viper that was run over by a truck.

The animals pretty much leave you alone in the camps, although we did have a scare one year. We'd noticed elephants hanging around near the camp, and I was told that because of the early rains, there was a certain fruit growing there that affected them like a narcotic.

Two Burger King franchise owners, Charlie Parton and Dick Daugherty, had bedded down and were almost asleep when they heard some noise alongside their tent. They'd probably had a few drinks, and their scene was like something out of Laurel and Hardy:

"Hey, Dick. Would you please quit scratching the tent?"

"I'm not scratching the tent."

"Well, who's making that noise?"

In the next moment, their tent was all but wiped out by a bull tusker rooting around for a piece of fruit the guys had left in there. (This is a no-no. Elephants don't see very well, but their sense of smell is phenomenal and can reach up to five miles, with the right wind.)

Dick and Charlie crawled out from under the crushed canvas while guides chased the elephant off with torches. Everybody was all right, but it was a close call—they could have been stepped on. Naturally, these guys took their fair share of ribbing for the remainder of the trip.

Another close call was on our 1987 trip when we were out on a lake in Rwanda looking at hippos. There was an enormous herd of hippos swimming out there, and we were all having a good time watching their antics. Our boat was a rickety old thing that looked like the *African Queen*, but we all laughed it off.

Just before we headed back toward shore, we veered over

to have a closer look at a mother and her baby—mostly to get some better pictures. (That's where you get in trouble; whenever you want a better picture, there's usually a risk factor to either animal or human.) When the mother disappeared underwater, I knew there was something wrong. Suddenly, the mother hippo came up under the boat and lifted the whole thing up on one side, about five feet into the air.

People went flying every which way, and one woman hanging over the edge taking pictures almost went overboard. She was halfway in the water when a couple of guys pulled her up. Then the hippo came and rammed a second

*H*ippos attacked our boat in Rwanda. Because they look so docile, tourists approach them with too little caution, and in Kenya alone they have killed several tourists in the last two years. (Suzi Hanna)

time, but she didn't get us that good, since we were already backing up—I figured we'd better call it a day.

There were a few minor cuts and scratches, but I don't even want to think about what would have happened if that boat had capsized. Hippos don't eat meat, but who wants to meet up with them in the water when they're mad?

∧∧

Probably the most spectacular part of any visit to the Dark Continent (for me anyway) is viewing the mountain gorillas of Rwanda. For many reasons, it's a very difficult proposition.

Obtaining permits—and you must have a permit—usually has to be done two years ahead of time. The Rwandan government is very strict about this and gives only one- and two-day permits. There are no rain checks, and it can get awfully stormy up there at an altitude of 10,000 to 12,000 feet. Trackers will help your group locate a gorilla family, but there are no guarantees. There can be hours of climbing involved in trailing the gorillas, and if people aren't in shape and can't keep up, they have to drop back.

One of the biggest disappointments in my life was on my first visit to the Virunga range, where the planet's last 400 or so mountain gorillas live. I'd read all the books and waited two years for the permit. I'd been to Africa a half dozen times already, but this particular excursion I'd been looking forward to all my life. But even with all our planning, we screwed up somewhere. On arrival at the base camp, we discovered we had only twelve permits for fourteen people.

The officials would not budge on this, but the people in our group insisted that I go, that I was the tour director and all that—that the rest would draw straws or something. I wouldn't even discuss it; Suzi and I wouldn't go and that was it. Suzi was very, very upset, but I told her not to worry—we'd be back.

We went back the following year, and this time, with a few dropouts, we wound up with an extra eight two-day permits. Isn't that the way it always goes? Anyway, on the first day, it was very hot, and we had to hike a long way through some stinging nettles. Our reward was to see a big silverback lying on a thick jungle bed in an open area. He didn't do much, but it was totally mesmerizing just to watch him for an hour or so. Here was the real king of the jungle, just resting on the grass. It was a magnificent sight—words fail you on this.

But the next day was even better. After about an hour's

These mountain gorillas are truly gentle giants and have never been known to harm man. Nevertheless, they are still hunted by poachers. This photo was taken in Rwanda, not far from where Dian Fossey did her pioneering studies. (Harold Squire)

hike under a beautiful, clear blue sky, we caught up to a gorilla family of about a dozen members playing in a bamboo thicket. This was what I'd always dreamed of seeing—gorillas of all ages swinging in the trees above us.

We all got very quiet and still. I'll never forget the lady next to me. She had all this camera equipment, but she was too enthralled to take a picture. She just couldn't do it. There was a gorilla overhead who relieved himself all over her, but she didn't move. I remember thinking, lady, you don't have to sit there while this gorilla's peeing all over you, but she didn't care. She was a real sport. This was the most fascinating experience she'd ever had, as it was for all of us.

The gorillas were having a blast. We'd caught them when they were playing, especially the youngsters, who were within two or three feet of us. Every so often the big male would look at you very sternly, and you'd look away, the way you're supposed to, so that there's no confrontation. Then he'd go back and sit down. You're the boss, boss.

The experience was beyond anything I'd ever imagined. The gorillas are habituated to people, which was one of the late Dian Fossey's great concerns. The fact that they allow people so close had contributed over the years to some of their deaths at the hands of poachers.

Some of the camera shots in *Gorillas in the Mist* (the movie based on Dian Fossey's book about her eighteen years living with the mountain gorillas) provide a remarkably close approximation of the experience of watching the gorillas in the wild. Dian Fossey visited the Columbus Zoo not long before she died, and while she disapproved of zoos in general, she was impressed with our gorilla families and the work by our keepers in the Ape House. She was also very anti-tourist, yet at the same time she came to recognize the fact that tourism has helped make the survival of the mountain gorillas a worldwide concern.

∧∧

One of the saddest facts of the animal world today is that we're running out of rhinos. This magnificent beast, who has been on the earth for 60 million years, may not have any predators, but he does have one natural enemy: man.

It takes just a few trips to Africa to personally witness the decline. In 1969, there were about 18,000 black rhinos in Kenya; by 1983 the number was down to 1,500—today there are fewer than 200, many on private sanctuaries. Unless you manage to get clearance to visit one of those, you probably won't ever see a black rhino.

The decline of the five remaining species of rhino in this century is directly attributable to poaching. In the Middle East, rhino horn is highly sought after for its decorative qualities, mostly for dagger handles; in the Far East, the horn is ground into powder and used medicinally or as an aphrodisiac. The price on the black market can run as high as $10,000 a kilo.

Today, the Kenyan government has gone to great lengths to stop poaching, and to a large extent they've succeeded, as far as the black rhino is concerned. But it may be too late. If we don't do something to increase their population, the black rhino may not last this century.

On one of my first trips to East Africa, I stayed at a camp on a large cattle ranch in Kenya that belonged to David and Delia Craig, an English couple who began offering tourist safaris fifteen years ago. It was there that I met Anna Mertz, a most fantastic person, who had dedicated her life to the preservation of the rhinoceros.

Anna Mertz is a hardy Englishwoman in her sixties who does not like publicity and does not talk much about what she does. Through the Craigs, I found out that she had spent the last of her savings to put up a $400,000 electrified fence on 10,000 acres that they had donated for a rhino sanctuary. The primary purpose of the fence is to keep elephants out; poachers have broken through this fence more than once to try to get to her animals, so you can imagine what they'll do in the wild.

In October 1988, the last five white rhinos in Kenya were shot to death by poachers on a heavily guarded reserve located only a short distance from Anna's rhino sanctuary. Several game wardens were killed trying to protect these animals who were very acclimated to humans. The horns from these five rhinos probably brought $150,000 on the black market.

On the sanctuary, Anna Mertz spends her days caring for and observing her twelve rhinos. Rhinos are very solitary animals, and getting them to breed is next to impossible. In small numbers, free-ranging males just can't find the females at the right time. Anna Mertz's studies on rhino behavior are one of the last hopes we have, or I should say, they have.

Anna was very leery of me at first, just as she is of all strangers. She has six African guards to protect 10,000 acres—each is assigned to two rhinos—and the only help she's interested in receiving is in the form of donations. She's a listener, not a talker, which might have helped us in the long run, since I'm just the opposite.

Since some of my wildlife trips were geared to one-hour TV specials for WCMH in Columbus, I thought, why not do a special just on the rhino? Anna agreed to participate when she realized that I wanted to do this to help people become aware of the rhino's plight, and for no other reason. From then on, we became good friends.

*A*nna Mertz is leading the charge to save the black rhino. Here we are on her 10,000-acre rhino sanctuary in Kenya. (Kathy Bruno)

We filmed that special, "The Last Rhino," in 1985—half tracking the efforts of anti-poaching units in Kenya's parks and the other half following Anna Mertz in her rhino reserve. It was a very powerful documentary, and I think we got our message across, even if we reached only a small fraction of the people we needed to reach. (Toward this end, my good friend and attorney, Vince Rakestraw, and I helped organize Rhino Rescue, Inc., a nonprofit organization whose efforts go solely to helping Anna Mertz's work on her ranch. I'm very proud of the people of central Ohio whose donations help support this woman out in the middle of Africa who's devoted her life to saving a beautiful animal from extinction.) Andy Lodge and Dan Hunt, keepers at our zoo, have raised over $40,000 for Anna's rhino sanctuary, with help from staff and volunteers, selling "Save a Horny Friend" T-shirts.

While we were there shooting the special, Anna had a six-month-old rhino named Samia that she'd hand-raised on a bottle. The baby had been abandoned by its mother and had become totally dependent on Anna, to the point of following her everywhere, even trying to get in bed with her.

Pope John Paul II was about to visit Africa at the time, and the Kenyan government wanted Anna to bring a young rhino for him to bless, as a representative of all wildlife. She didn't want to do it, for fear that the trip—they would have to travel by plane to the Masai Mara—might harm Samia. She was adamantly against it and told me so. She said it was unfair to put that stress on the animal.

Well, my PR wheels were turning about a mile a minute. What better way to publicize a species' struggle for survival than to have it blessed by one of the most powerful men in the world? I talked to her about it for half an hour, telling her that I understood her fears for the animal's health, but also that she had to balance the potential harm to Samia against all the good that would come from people all over the world learning about the rhino. She saw my point and agreed to do it.

On the big day, they flew Sammy to see the Pope. With the Pope standing there, Sammy tried to take off; maybe the Pope moved wrong or something. Anyway, the Pope did get to within a few feet of her, blessed her and said a few words about how this beautiful animal is virtually extinct and how the entire world must share the burden of God's endangered creatures. So I guess I did my share in helping to bring the Pope together with the rhino.

As far as tourism goes, Africa is changing rapidly year by year. Almost all the wildlife today is confined to huge national parks like Tsavo, which has approximately 5,000 square miles. It has to be this way to protect the animals.

*S*ammy the rhino at age two weeks.
(Suzi Hanna)

One of the greatest ways to see wildlife is by hot-air balloon. It ain't cheap ($200 to $300), but it's worth every penny. You have to get up very early, about four o'clock, which is the best time for a safari anyway. My groups don't go at that hour, because not everyone wants to get up that early for whatever reason.

The balloons are blown up and launched just as the sun's coming up over the Serengeti Plain. The animals don't seem to hear anything, and you're right there just fifty feet above them. Then they'll take the balloons up to a thousand feet or so and back down over roaming herds of wildebeest, antelopes, dik-dik, giraffes, lions— they're all out there early in the morning.

For two hours, you soar over these animals, seeing them in numbers, seeing animal kills and much more. The quiet up there is something else. Then you come back down, walk about a hundred yards and have a champagne breakfast under the acacia trees. There may be better ways to spend money, but I can't think of any.

If I couldn't be a zoo director, I think I'd like to be a tour guide in Africa. I'd never get tired of the wildlife, and I get a great thrill out of being a part of people's first experiences on safari.

You see a great change in the people coming back from Africa. They've seen things they've never imagined they'd see in their lifetimes, and they're more humble, more serene. They haven't really had a vacation; they've had an educational experience. They're up all day from dawn to dusk seeing new things.

When we arrive back home, most people are exhausted and happy to see their families. They'll quickly resume their normal routines and appreciate the little things—a fast-food burger, clean clothes, a cold beer, whatever. But then it's only a matter of days before someone will call me from his office and say, "Hey, Jack. I was just thinking about how great it was over there, how I wish we were back over there right now . . ."

Elephant damage on a huge baobab tree in Botswana. The tree is over one thousand years old, one of the oldest trees in the world. (Suzi Hanna)

16

CHINA
MISSION

To many zoo directors today, exhibiting (or even better, breeding) a giant panda would be the ultimate in zoological achievement. It's something like an art museum seeking a special Rembrandt—the collection may be great, but if they could only get that one painting. Imagine a museum borrowing the *Mona Lisa* for a few months; do you think it might bring a few art lovers out of the woodwork? That's about what the panda, even on a short-term loan, can mean to a zoo.

In 1986, we took a twelve-person Columbus delegation to visit China; among other goals, we visited the Kunming Zoo, where we signed a "sister zoo" agreement. Earlier, our mayor, Dana Rinehart, had approached a Chinese minister with the hope of exchanging "breeding technology," which was a polite way of opening negotiations for a panda loan. It was a nice idea, but the Chinese aren't about to exchange a pair of pandas for anything short of the state of Texas.

The trip was fascinating and successful, even if we didn't come home with pandas in hand, which would have been like coming home with the emperor's jewels. After much negotiating and observing of protocol, we did get a promise of a panda loan in 1992 (when the city will be commemorating the 500th anniversary of Christopher Columbus' arrival in the New World), along with an agreement for golden monkeys in 1988.

For me, the highlight of the trip was when the director of the Beijing Zoo offered to let me hold a giant panda cub. Cuddling with this little creature was like stepping on the moon—I was ready to go home; my trip was complete.

Anyone who's ever seen a giant panda in the flesh can easily understand the public's obsession with this animal. Despite their size, they're cute and adorable. I know it's a cliché, but they're like big stuffed toys. Pandas are fascinating to watch, but most importantly, they embody a playful innocence that human beings cherish. I hadn't realized that they're as popular in China as they are in the United States.

With fewer than 1,000 surviving in the wild, the giant panda has become a symbol for all endangered species; the struggle to save the giant panda has become a struggle to save all wildlife. The panda's primary enemies are poachers and loss of habitat. The animal's sole natural habitat is a rapidly diminishing region of bamboo forest in central China; a panda consumes up to forty pounds of the plant, its primary food source, daily. To complicate matters, bamboo goes through a periodic die-out, causing food shortages and starvation for some pandas. Pandas are also carnivores, but are generally too slow to catch prey. They are fragile animals in a fragile environment and face almost certain extinction if our commitment to their survival is halted in any way.

One of the biggest thrills of my life was when the director of the Beijing Zoo let me hold a giant panda cub. Even in China, the giant panda is a major attraction, and twelve million people visit the Beijing Zoo every year. (Suzi Hanna)

Recently, the scramble by zoos nationwide to borrow giant pandas from China has created considerable controversy. Borrowing is actually a loose term for renting, since some zoos have been known to pay up to $500,000 just to have them for thirty to ninety days. (They more than make up for this expense when "pandamania" hits, and large profits are realized on everything from admissions to T-shirts.)

Two issues have been raised: (1) Is the shuffling of the animals from zoo to zoo (and continent to continent) in any way endangering the survival of the species? (2) Are the funds generated by these "rentals" being properly applied toward conservation efforts by the Chinese? I personally feel the Chinese are trying to do their best to preserve the panda with what little resources they have to work with. In fact, I understand they have spent up to $25 million on panda conservation. How much have we in the United States spent in preserving our national emblem, the American bald eagle?

The overriding fear with the panda loans is that their breeding cycles—which are already quite mysterious—might be adversely affected by travel and environmental changes. The proposed guidelines, as established by the World Wildlife Fund (WWF) and other conservation groups, are that pandas between the prime breeding ages of six and fifteen should not be moved from their home zoos. In May 1988 these agencies came down very hard on the Toledo Zoo for allegedly accepting some breeding-age pandas from the Chinese. Now, if this is true, I'm sure it was unintentional. But even then, what are they supposed to do, send them back?

I think it would be a serious setback to put a permanent ban on panda loans, and I'm not just saying that because we hope to have them in 1992. The point is that panda loans have done much more good than harm in this country.

Pandas make people become instantly aware of conservation. People are profoundly affected when they see first-hand this lovable creature that might become extinct. The effect comes from seeing it up close and live, not on a slide, on film or in a book. I advocate extending the panda loan periods, so that more zoologists can further study their breeding habits and possibly come up with some answers.

Not just in Columbus—though I'd love for our people to have a chance to help them breed—but also in other zoos that have successful breeding programs. Meanwhile, we're anxiously awaiting our turn, if all goes well.

⋀⋀

The snub-nosed golden monkeys weren't going to be anywhere near the drawing card that giant pandas would be, we knew that. But still, they're extremely endangered—only a handful exist in captivity in the United States—they're quite beautiful and they're generally different from most primates. We were very happy with the Chinese offer. to "loan" us a pair for the summer of 1988, but little did I know how complicated it would be just to get them over to Columbus.

Several teams had to be sent to China to work out details; as we already knew, nothing is ever quick or easy over there. For the final negotiation, we sent one of our trustees, Jim McGuire, who's a lawyer and a very patient man. After eight days of constant talks, and eight days of overseas calling back to general manager Jerry Borin, Jim was totally spent, but he finally had a deal.

The fee for the monkeys was $40,000 for one hundred days, but that was just a start. We had to provide two animal studies scholarships to Ohio State—no problem there. We had to secure the import permit from the U.S. Fish and Wildlife Service, who were holding up all permits on exotics from China because of the panda situation—we needed assistance from Congressman Wylie on that one. We had to fly a delegation of Chinese over for the "opening" ceremony at the zoo—I got the airlines to help us with that. Plus we had to insure the monkeys for $400,000 each.

We had to build an exhibit acceptable to the Chinese. We had to arrange for an interpreter and boarding for the monkeys' keeper and veterinarian. I managed to have some rooms donated by a local motel, but our visitors wanted to be on zoo grounds. I can't say I blamed them; if anything ever happened to the monkeys, these gentlemen probably would have had to defect. So I had a mobile home loaned to us from a trailer park and that was fine. But then I had to find them some Chinese food—their kind. Needless to say, I couldn't locate any sea slugs in Columbus.

All in all, it was worth the effort. The monkeys, Zhuang-Zhuang and Jin-Yo, were magnificent specimens. They had exquisite golden hair that flowed down their backs and beautiful iridescent-blue faces. They were also fascinating to watch. They spent hours grooming each other into an immaculate state and the rest of the time taking long jumps around their exhibit. For their size, they were extremely agile. Best of all, they mated constantly, but I never got the results on that.

If the attendance surge wasn't quite what we might have expected for the monkeys, I think that might be because we're a little jaded with primate success in Columbus. The one hundred-plus temperatures (Zhuang-Zhuang and Jin-Yo enjoyed air conditioning, of course; otherwise they might not have made it) didn't help any. But I think the greatest benefit was how the golden monkeys and their keepers affected our zoo staff.

From the very first day, Mr. Wang, the keeper, and Dr. Lei, their veterinarian, made a big hit. They were extremely friendly and willing to work, and our appreciation grew as we saw how dedicated these men were to their animals—it was like they were guarding gold in Fort Knox.

The golden monkeys' stay ended with a "closing" ceremony that required the visit of another half dozen dignitaries from the People's Republic (and another airline deal), but I was half expecting that. By then, I was starting to get a handle on this protocol business, and we closed with a great deal of goodwill. But if we went to these extremes for a couple of golden monkeys, I only shudder to think what might lie ahead for the giant pandas.

Columbus Zoo, 1940. (Columbus Zoo file)

ZOOS—
THE
LAST
HOPE?

*W*hen I arrived in Columbus, "cage" had pretty much become a nasty word in the zoo world. Yet at the same time, Columbus still had North American cougars displayed next to primates in the gorilla house. That's an example of what I call the "menagerie effect"—accumulate all the animals you can and put 'em behind bars. Well, I'd had enough of that, and besides, people don't want to see animals behind bars. One of the great benefits of having animals outdoors is that it serves as a reminder of our rich wildlife heritage in the world today and how we're in danger of losing it.

Since the turn of the century, animal habitats have been rapidly disappearing everywhere in the world. It's common knowledge that it is man's progress that poses the greatest threat to the animal world, which is now losing species at a very alarming rate. Nearly a thousand species of plants and animals approach extinction each year. This number may increase tenfold in the nineties, reaching 10,000 species a year. That's one species per hour! Zoos, which thirty years ago represented a small part of the problem by taking animals from the wild, have today become part of the solution.

Thanks to zoological advances, captive animals today increasingly enjoy natural habitats where they can develop and flourish. Zoos continue to improve and to meet the particular needs of diverse groups of animals, with the ultimate hope that they may breed and further their species. Captive breeding programs have saved such species as the Asiatic wild horse, the Arabian oryx, Père David's deer, the American bison, the Hawaiian goose and hopefully the well-publicized California condor from extinction.

It's a mixed blessing for me to have had the experience of being the director of a very old zoo in Florida, along with being a board member of an equally old zoo in Knoxville, before coming to Columbus. My main job at both places was to raise money and raise awareness so that they could continue to exist. That experience gave me a good perspective of the way things used to be in the zoo world versus how they are today. We've come a long way.

When people think of working at a zoo, one automatically thinks of a career in zoology, veterinary medicine, research, education or zookeeping. However, in today's modern zoo there could be as many as sixteen different careers involved in the entire operation. No zoo can operate efficiently without a good maintenance staff, public relations and marketing personnel, grounds crew, multimedia professionals, financial and accounting staff, dietitians, group sales, concessions, publications, fund-raising, office personnel, ride operators, ticket takers, and the list goes on. So the opportunity to work in a zoological park can be approached in many ways.

The dawn of each day at the zoo presents new adventures, new challenges. Many of these challenges turn out to be medical in nature, and our veterinarians must often be highly creative in meeting them. Did you know, for example, that it is almost impossible to determine the sex of a hyena? That human birth-control pills work on a gorilla? That Preparation H may help in reducing a growth on a snake?

Two challenges in 1988 were successfully met with good results for the animals involved. The secretary bird is a long-legged, ground-dwelling carnivorous African bird that spends much of its time in the wild stomping on vegetation to flush out small reptiles and insects for lunch. Even though they are not great fliers, captive secretary birds must be pinioned if they are to be exhibited in open yards. Pinioning is a surgical procedure on the wing that requires anesthesia followed by recovery in a contained area so that the bird remains quiet and doesn't thrash around. Despite these precautions, one of our birds did thrash and broke a leg, which didn't heal after being pinned for several months. The leg had to be amputated, and the search was on for a suitable prosthesis. After trial and error, the right fit and attachment was found, and he now moves about his yard almost as good as new. However, exercise and feather growth on the upper leg sometimes cause his leg to work loose. On those days, it is unnerving to hear the transmission on our radio system: "The secretary bird's leg has fallen off again!"

Secretary bird with artificial leg. (Columbus Zoo, Nancy Staley)

Another patient in 1988 was a ten-month-old polar bear, Blizzard, who delighted visitors all summer long with her antics. By summer's end, just when she was scheduled to move on to a new home at the Indianapolis Zoo, she slipped on algae in a puddle and fell eighteen feet into her exhibit moat. Mom Zero dived into the moat at Blizzard's first cry and refused to leave her injured offspring. Both had to be tranquilized to rescue the youngster, who, it turned out, had fractured two bones in her left hind leg.

In addition to our own veterinarians, we are fortunate to have the services of the Ohio State University School of Veterinary Medicine at our disposal, and their team of specialists quickly set to work. Since the bear probably would not have tolerated a cast, they repaired the bones with stainless-steel plates attached by metal screws. By the next day, Blizzard was up and limping and was walking well within days. After about seven weeks of recovery, our Blizzard blew into Indianapolis to a beautiful new habitat with a handsome young male bear awaiting her arrival. I do hope, however, that Blizzard's offspring won't follow in their mother's footsteps—down into the moat.

A few years ago, a young zebra wasn't so fortunate. Squiggly may have been born prematurely—at least his chest and front leg muscles were too underdeveloped to support him, and they didn't strengthen. The veterinarians tried everything—slings, casts, splints, you name it. An army of staff and volunteers worked with the little guy day and night. He became a cause. They bottle-fed him, coaxed corn, one kernel at a time, into his mouth. They massaged those legs, walked him to exercise them and slept with him in his stall night after night. If love and determination could have saved Squiggly, he would be here today. But as his body grew, his muscles didn't. The time came when we knew, for Squiggly's sake and for those humans who were so involved with him, that the struggle must be humanely ended. We didn't win that one, but there was reward in having tried.

*S*quiggly the zebra, born prematurely, was unable to walk. We tried everything from slings to casts to get him on his feet with limited success. Exotic veterinary medicine is a very new field. (Columbus Dispatch)

Exotic veterinary medicine is still a relatively new field; our doctors constantly exchange information with other zoos, but sometimes they must break new ground because no research or precedent exists. This is one of the most exciting and growing areas in the zoo world today as we try to maintain and improve the health of our animals and, beyond that, try to find ways to enable endangered species to reproduce. But whether the animal is a common bunny in the outreach collection or an endangered snow leopard or rhino, it receives the same quality of medical care from our vets and keepers and the cadre of specialists who are unfailingly available to us from around our community.

Back in the early 1970s, the U.S. Department of Agriculture finally began to clamp down on the zoos and animal parks that did not conform to USDA standards—either clean up your act or we'll close you down. Also, as more and more modern zoos opened with spacious quarters and attractive, well-designed habitats, old-style zoos with their cramped cages and depressing conditions became less and less accepted by the public.

Propagating the species was not the primary purpose of the old zoos. Sure, if an animal could breed, that was fine. But the main idea was to obtain as many species as possible to exhibit to the general public. Don't worry about the conditions, just show the animal. For example, if a zoo director had a male spotted hyena, rather than get a female, he might be more concerned with getting a striped hyena. That way he could say he now had a spotted *and* a striped hyena. He could have an Asian *and* an African lion, a Siberian *and* a Bengal tiger, etc.

One of the first things I did in Columbus was to take inventory and decide which animals would have to go, through either donations or sales to other zoos. I'm sure I surprised some people, but the purpose was to relieve overcrowding, to give our other animals more room. You have to look at the overall picture.

Zoos today have become more specialized. In Columbus, we know what our strengths are. We do well with gorillas, American bald eagles, polar bears, lesser pandas, cheetahs, and cichlid fish, to name a few. We're also very good with reptiles. We don't get involved with breeding sea mammals because we're not equipped to do so. We don't have a major bird collection right now because we don't have the proper facilities. I've taken some criticism on that, but until we have a proper aviary—and this could cost a million dollars or more—we won't have many birds here. Some zoos are known for their penguin collections, some for their giant tortoises. I think the trend today of going with your strengths is a good one, and it's the animals who are the winners in the long run.

Just the feeding of animals alone has changed in many ways in recent years. I mentioned earlier the outstanding diet that our gorillas enjoy—diets go a long way toward ensuring breeding success. But it's also what the animals don't eat at the zoo that can be very important.

In the old days, people were encouraged to feed the animals. This led to a great deal of abuse. Today, zoos go to great lengths to stop public feeding. When I was little, back in the 1950s, you took bread to feed the ducks, you took bananas and raisins for the monkeys, peanuts for the elephants, whatever. It was fun, but it was wrong.

Indiscriminate feeding can give the animals improper nutrition and unnatural behaviors. Having bears sit up on their back legs to beg for marshmallows is neither natural nor educational. It's taken a while, but we're finally starting to get the point across.

We prohibit public feeding of the animals, as, among other problems, it causes unnatural behavior, like this polar bear "begging." (Columbus Zoo file)

Another sad result of public feeding is all the nonorganic items we've pulled from animals' stomachs—plastic bags, all sorts of coins, glass bottles, etc. Sometimes, these have been fatal. At the Columbus Zoo we have a display with an assortment of the things we've found inside animals (after autopsies) that we call "the museum of human stupidity." One look at it is self-explanatory.

On a more positive note, we, like many other zoos, have established a successful "Adopt an Animal" program, which allows the public to share in the cost of feeding animals. Individuals, schools or even corporate or civic groups can sponsor any single animal at the zoo. Annual feeding costs can vary from a high of $4,015 for an Asian elephant to a low of $20 for a shovel-nosed tree frog.

Recently we've added a "Plant Parenthood" program, in which donors can support the extensive botanical projects at the Columbus Zoo. Zoo visitors have come to expect beautiful gardens. In 1978, we had two floral gardens with maybe three hundred half-wilted flowers—today we have

The cages that held our lions and tigers for almost 30 years... (Columbus Zoo file)

over a hundred gardens and sixty thousand flowers. Steve Beard and Tedd Kerr, our two dedicated horticulturists, grow everything from seed in three greenhouses on the zoo grounds.

We have 142 acres to care for with approximately one hundred genera and two hundred species of trees and shrubs, valued at $2.5 million. A staff of six people works day and night to provide a beautiful setting for both our visitors and our animal collection.

In addition to beautification, zoo flora plays an important part in the design of natural habitats—what we call "furniture for the animals." You can't just put a fence around some land and call it a natural habitat—you have to try to approximate the animals' home turf the best you can. You provide trees, shrubs, grass, ponds and even rocky hiding places. It's phenomenal what some zoos have done in this vein, to the point of creating virtual jungles and rain forests in the middle of metropolitan areas.

... became the new lion exhibit—without bars. (Columbus Zoo file)

Our old giraffe pens... (Columbus Zoo, Nancy Staley)

The old elephant building and yard... (Columbus Zoo, Earl W. Smith III)

... and our new giraffe habitat. (Columbus Zoo, Nancy Staley)

... became the gorilla habitat. (Columbus Zoo file)

This quote may be overused in the zoo world, but that's because it so clearly defines part of what zoos today are all about.

In the end, we will conserve only what we love, we will love only what we know, and we will know only what we are taught.

BABA DIOM
SENEGAL

Why even have zoos at all? The question comes up often enough, and I don't resent it. There are many reasons for the existence of zoos, but in my mind, four important

"ZooKids" gives preschoolers a weekly close-up experience of the zoo. (Columbus Zoo, Nancy Staley)

At the zoo, kids can learn about animals up close and personal. Here a group tries on pants made to Bongo the gorilla's actual size. (Columbus Zoo, Nancy Staley)

points always stand out: conservation, education, research and recreation.

More than 120 million people will visit zoos every year in the United States and Canada—more than the combined attendance of baseball, football and hockey. Most of these people are simply seeking a recreational experience that can't be found anywhere else. Zoos afford them the opportunity to enjoyably experience animals firsthand. People can read great books or watch well-made wildlife television specials, but nothing replaces the direct impact of seeing a living, breathing creature that one wouldn't ordinarily see.

Today, zoos are conservationists. We breed animals, both to propagate species that are often endangered and to provide animals for our own and other zoos—again, we rarely capture them in the wild anymore. Returning animals to the wild is an altruistic and utopian concept that, in our lifetimes, can realistically happen in only a very few instances. So, since every animal born in a zoo will probably die there, we, as caretakers, owe that animal the best life possible.

Having animals in captivity has helped us to learn much about their health, reproductive and environmental needs. With the gene pool so limited in many instances, zoological research has enabled us to make great advances in areas such as embryo transfers that will help save nearly extinct species. With apes, thousands of hours of just plain watching qualifies as valid research toward learning more about their social habits, which, in turn, will further their species.

The educational side to zoos is a never-ending process, particularly with regard to children, who learn not only about the habits and ways of animals they're seeing for the first time but also about endangered and threatened species. What they're gaining is an awareness we hope they'll carry with them the rest of their lives.

Here at the Columbus Zoo, we have three buildings containing nine classrooms, an auditorium and video capabilities to accommodate several hundred children per day. Our classes include "Zooper Saturdays" for youngsters ages three to six; "ZooKids," which is taught every weekday for preschoolers; "Night Owl Camp-Ins" for groups such as Boy Scouts, Girl Scouts, church groups, etc., in which they actually spend the night on the zoo grounds; "Summer Experience," which is a camp for two thousand young people during the summer months; "Zoofari Outreach," a program in which we take animals and educational material to the schools; "Wildlife Art" classes for both kids and adults; and an "Adult Lecture Series," in which international experts in wildlife such as Jean Michel Cousteau, the late Dian Fossey and many more have spoken. A staff of fourteen certified teachers do a great job with all these "little critters."

Good signage and good graphics play a vital role in zoo education. Graphics will tell you where the animals are from, what they eat, how many remain, their migrations, etc. When I visit a zoo, I often look at the graphics before I even look at the animal.

In Columbus, we have docents, volunteers who form the backbone of our educational program. These volunteers all have to take a series of classes, after which they become certified for their many areas of work. Docents donate thousands of hours to the zoo, teaching, answering visitors' questions, leading tours for the blind or handicapped, protecting animals, watching for births and organizing events, just to name a few of their activities. If we had to pay them even the minimum wage, the work they do would add up to hundreds of thousands of dollars annually.

The zoo has numerous employee classifications—full-time, part-time, seasonal, volunteer—but one of our more unusual categories is "community service." As a public institution, we have the option of cooperating with the courts to provide a work site for individuals convicted of nonviolent crimes who are assigned community service in lieu of jail or prison. We get all types, from indigents to corporate executives who have run afoul of the law. In fact, the zoo may be one of the preferred places to serve, with people imagining themselves in up-close and personal contact with the animals. They are supervised by our security staff, which works with the courts, makes the work assignments and so on.

Not long ago, the owner of two vicious dogs that had attacked and killed a two-year-old girl was sentenced to eighty hours of service at the zoo—as the judge said, "to learn the nature of vicious animals." I don't know exactly which vicious animals the judge had in mind, because our community service workers don't get anywhere near our collection. They mostly wash golf carts and windows and help on the grounds, raking, picking up litter and sweeping, but we are grateful for their help and happy to work with other community institutions.

Naturally, I consider television an important educational tool for wildlife. My taking animals on shows such as *Good*

Morning America and *Late Night with David Letterman* has become a bone of contention among my critics in the zoo world. They say that I'm showboating, that I'm misrepresenting wildlife, that the alien conditions cause the animals undue stress and that these trips generally serve little purpose. I couldn't disagree more.

Entertainment-oriented shows reach large audiences, audiences that might not be in tune with the worldwide wildlife situation. If we can catch the attention of the millions of young people who watch the Letterman show, we can gain converts to the role of conservation. The national exposure of well-known television personalities endorsing our zoos is invaluable, and the live animals that appear on the tube are our best salesmen.

As for the animals, they are only chosen for travel after my joint consultation with keepers, curators, an animal management committee and veterinarians. They're checked thoroughly before they leave and upon their return. They are not greatly stressed, and I will even venture to say that the animals we choose may even enjoy their appearances away from the zoo. In ten years of traveling with Columbus Zoo animals, not one has ever been harmed.

As for those who criticize my methods as being unscientific, well, I just don't think that most of the general public is interested in the scientific approach, especially on programs that are geared to entertain. And on this, I will reiterate my personal credo, as adapted from the words of Walt Disney: "I'd rather entertain and hope people learn, than teach and hope people are entertained."

∧∧

Today, more than a thousand species are in danger of extinction. For some endangered species, breeding in captivity is their last chance. Of course, we'd rather preserve them in the wild, but with the worldwide rate of destruction of animal habitats, this is often impossible. We are losing twenty-five to fifty acres of tropical rain forest every sixty seconds due to woodcutting for agriculture, roads, etc. In six months, that becomes an area the size of the state of

Ohio. Plants and animals yet to be discovered and named are becoming extinct. In the next forty years, some 600,000 to one million species are expected to vanish. At one time, our national bird came very close to extinction; there are fewer than one hundred fifty grizzly bears left in the lower forty-eight states; only twenty or so Florida panthers remain alive; the California condor is virtually extinct. However, thanks to the San Diego Zoo and the Los Angeles Zoo, it may have a chance for survival.

The Species Survival Plan (SSP) was recently implemented by the American Association of Zoological Parks and Aquariums toward the goal of ensuring diversified gene pools of selected endangered species. There are currently more than forty species on the SSP list, each with its own captive breeding strategy and an accompanying long-term support system.

The member institutions of the AAZPA participate in a coordinated effort by moving animals around from zoo to zoo on the basis of these long-term strategies. Over 60,000 animals in participating zoos have been inventoried by

Elephant herd during a storm in Kenya. (Suzi Hanna)

computer so that the best choices can be made for individual breeding programs. At our fingertips we have the age, sex, parentage, place of birth or even circumstances of death of any of these animals.

Currently, among the animals the Columbus Zoo has out on SSP breeding loans are red pandas, Bengal tigers, Grévy's zebras, cheetahs and a chimpanzee. Among those on loan to us are a white rhinoceros, an Asian elephant, a Puerto Rican crested toad and eight gorillas. We also know that one, maybe both, of our gorilla twins will probably eventually be introduced into a family group in some other zoo. Parting with animals that have become zoo family over the years can be tough, but we all agree that these are necessary steps if handled in an appropriate and fair manner.

A poached African elephant in Kenya, killed for his ivory tusks. Poaching is sickening, but sadly not uncommon. (Suzi Hanna)

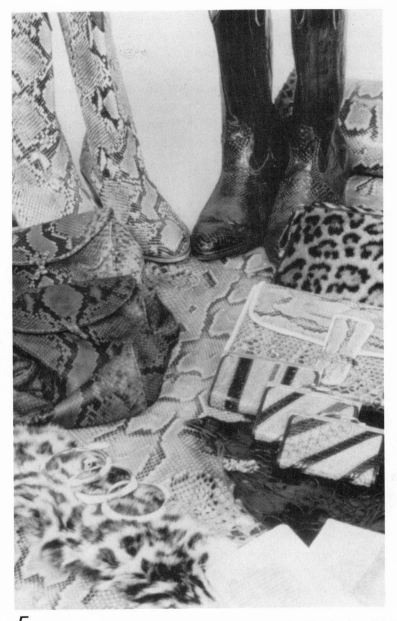

Exotic animal products—their sale only encourages poaching in the wild.
(Columbus Zoo, Tim Williams)

Animals are classified "endangered" when they exist in unusually small numbers, when their death rate exceeds their birth rate and when their natural environments can no longer provide for their needs. Animals are classified "threatened" when they exist in small numbers, even though their habitats could potentially support larger numbers. The reasons for any animal's habitat problems can vary from strip mining to deforestation to swamp drainage. In the United States we lose about 500,000 acres of wetlands each year.

In most instances, mankind is usually the enemy. Overgrazing of livestock has resulted in soil erosion and useless, barren land; illegal hunting and capture has drastically reduced some animal groups; recreational vehicles and motorboats have damaged habitats; commercial expansion—highways, pipelines, housing, etc.—has destroyed habitats and disrupted important migratory routes.

There are many ways that everyone can help. Just by spreading the word about the problem and how people contribute to it will go a long way toward changing the way people behave. In the Far East, it is still generally considered an acceptable luxury to wear certain hides or furs from endangered animals—a snow leopard coat can cost up to $30,000.

But most importantly, people should simply not buy exotic animal products, whether the animal is endangered or not. In 1979, there were 1.3 million elephants in Africa; by 1988, fewer than 750,000 remained. To meet the current demand, nearly 70,000 must die each year. Of those that remain, youngsters die without their mothers and the social and learning systems are broken down. Almost every form of ivory trade is strictly forbidden, but over 80 percent of the ivory circulating today is illegal. Even if you are buying ivory that is legal—say from African elephants that have been "cropped" (to control overpopulation)—you are encouraging others to buy illegal African ivory and ivory from the highly endangered Asian elephant. The same thing is true with ostrich skin and snakeskin for belts and boots:

trade in these is legal, but it promotes the exploitation of exotic animals in general. Alligators have only just made it back up to the "threatened" class (up from "endangered") thanks to our conservation efforts. There may be 700,000 African elephants left, but it's highly disturbing to see stores promoting and people buying elephant-skin golf bags; we've got plenty of good synthetics for such purposes.

Now, I'm not saying people shouldn't eat meat or should wear rubber shoes. I'm not a fanatic. And although I've never really hunted, I've always respected controlled hunting and hunters. My brother Bush is an avid hunter and an avid conservationist, as most hunters are. "He kills 'em, and Jack saves 'em," my dad likes to say.

Even on the level of big game in East Africa, controlled hunting has protected wildlife. With a loss of predators, hunters have for years been called on to control overpopulated herds. This is particularly true with the white-tailed deer in North America, where there are no large numbers of great predators left, except for man. Hunting license fees generate considerable amounts of income for conservation projects. Ducks Unlimited is a perfect example of an international hunting organization that has saved millions of acres of Canadian wetlands for ducks to breed on.

Again, everybody can help by sharing concern for all wildlife. Ignorance, not malice, is often the problem. By removing the demand for exotic animal products, we can all help eliminate the incentives for poaching, illegal trade and the loss of wildlife.

We may be able to survive in a world where the giant panda, the California condor and the black rhino exist only as pictures in a book. But do we want to? The choice is ours.

*A*nimals, even timber wolves, whether they know it or not, give people a big lift.
(Columbus Zoo, Earl W. Smith III)

JAIL END

To laugh often and much, to win the respect of intelligent people and affection of children, to earn the appreciation of honest critics and endure the betrayal of false friends, to appreciate beauty, to find the best in others, to leave the world a bit better whether by a healthy child, a garden patch or a redeemed social condition; to know even one life has breathed easier because you have lived. This is to have succeeded.

—Ralph Waldo Emerson

How do you measure success, in a life, in a career? Not a day goes by that I don't ask myself: Is this the right way to go? Am I doing the right thing? Not just in the routine decision making of being a zoo director but with the overall picture in mind.

Back when I was selling real estate in Knoxville or trying to promote a wilderness movie, I knew it wasn't the right direction for me. When I first got to Columbus, it was like the weight of not knowing what to do was lifted right off my shoulders—my life opened up again; it took on a purpose, just in the everyday business at hand.

Being on national TV is gratifying, and I'm sure many people measure success this way, the same with being recognized on the street. But when I reflect on my career, it's the less obvious things that have given me the most satisfaction. The times when animals gave people a big lift, and I could say I did my part.

Several years ago, I received a request from an instructor at an Ohio penitentiary for a bird donation. I sent some parrots and that started a whole new program within that prison. The instructor wrote to tell me how much taking care of the animals—today they have deer, rabbits and guinea pigs—helped rehabilitate prisoners, how it made them more compassionate. Who else could empathize more with an enclosed animal than a prisoner?

There's a young mentally retarded woman who spends a lot of her time at the Columbus Zoo. The animals make her happy—it's as simple as that. She may say things that make little sense to the rest of us and she may think the animals are listening to her, but doctors and nurses can't provide what she gets from the animals.

In 1986, I visited a twelve-year-old girl suffering from encephalitis in a Houston hospital. I took some young animals to her bedside, and something special happened between the two of us and those animals that day. I will always treasure this letter that I later received from her:

May 14, 1986

Dear Jack,

You were great on the David Letterman show and I will be watching for you on *Good Morning America*. Mom and I have taped your shows so far.

I just wanted to let you know the doctors changed my medication about 2 weeks ago and I don't have the Parkinson shakes. I am learning to walk on my knees and am pretty good at it. I had to give up on crawling because I am still weak in my arms. Since the medication change, my appetite is better and I have gained 6 pounds. I weigh 74 pounds now.

Since the medicine has stopped my shakes, I have been taking animal pictures with my new camera. Thanks to you and your kindness. The zoo calendar you sent has inspired my interest in animal photography. I am going to the Houston Zoo soon to practice my photography from the wheelchair view.

I want you to know that I would probably still be in bed if you hadn't come along to perk me up. I was labeled a "medical challenge," but you helped me more than any doctor could. Someday I will walk again. Mom is always saying, "Let's practice walking for Jack so that you can let him know." I do practice every day!

Tell your daughter hi for me and I hope she is doing okay. Has she ever heard of encephalitis? I hadn't until I got it.

See you soon on TV. (Please write.)

Your special friend,
Kristen Dixon

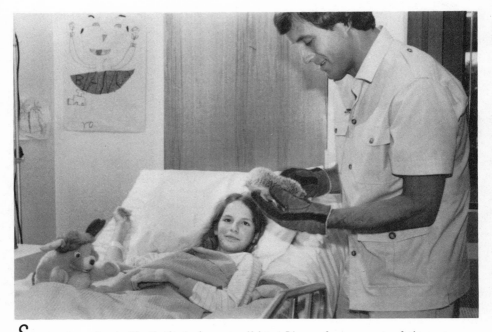

*S*ome young animals, like the hedgehog, gave Kristen Dixon a few moments of pleasure and relief. (Jack Hanna)

Then, for the first time in my life, I really knew what Emerson meant when he said, ". . . to know even one life has breathed easier because you have lived." Kristen not only walked again but today she is leading a healthy, normal life. I only wish more children could experience the joy and inspiration of God's creatures.

So despite the frantic pace of public appearances and the notoriety of television, these are some of the things that really count for me—personally seeing animals making a difference in the lives of those who are less fortunate. And it goes on everywhere, not just at Columbus but at many

*F*eeding Noah the moose. (Columbus Dispatch, Tom Dodge)

other zoos. I've seen it time and time again. By sharing, we receive so much more than we give, and that's really the bottom line for me.

But what of the future? I know that animals will always be an important part of my life, that I will always want to share their magic with other people and that I will always care about what happens to wildlife. But getting back to answering the big questions, maybe every person needs some sort of refuge or hideaway to think about them.

In October 1987, I was invited out West by a young enthusiastic zoo director, Jim Duncan. He wanted me to do a fund-raiser for Zoo Montana, a civic organization in Billings that's trying to establish a zoo. So far they have over 2,400 members, but no zoo. I'm sure they'll have one soon; they're a dedicated group.

Anyway, on my first visit ever to Montana, I fell in love with the state, the people, the mountains, all the Big Sky country. Almost right away, I decided to purchase a lot and build a cabin on some land adjoining Custer National Forest. At first, I only planned to make it a vacation retreat for my family and me, but after a few trips out there, I thought, this is where I have to live.

I became just as excited about seeing natural wildlife in Montana as I had in Africa—in a way, more so, since we have so little of it left. Within two or three visits, I'd already seen a mountain lion, a black bear, loads of bighorn sheep, moose, golden eagles, grouse, beavers, otters and a host of other animals, large and small.

The cabin I built is two hours from Billings by car, thirty-two miles from Yellowstone National Park by horseback. The land is on a large ranch owned by an avid outdoorsman named Ribs Mikelson. At an elevation of 5,000 feet, it lies at the base of Cathedral Mountain and overlooks the Stillwater Valley. From my porch, the idyllic view over the Stillwater River is hardly changed from what it must have been like 150 years ago. Only the bison and the Indians are missing.

*M*ontana Hanna and Magoo in a Bear Creek saloon. (Suzi Hanna)

I hope Montana never gets discovered, at least in the sense that states like Colorado and Arizona have. I know the economy is quite depressed there, but the ultimate life for me, even if it's just fantasy at this point, would be to work with wildlife in a national park as a ranger.

I do have a contract in Columbus (through 1992), but I

don't have a crystal ball. Who knows, maybe someday I won't have to worry about rain on weekends, a visitor getting belted by Koko the elephant, the going price for hay or whether the zoo concessions are selling enough hot dogs. Maybe my only worry will be feeding my Madagascar cockroaches. Then I'll be able to just step off my front porch into one of the greatest zoos in the hemisphere. Maybe then, instead of Jungle Jack, I will become Montana Hanna.

PHOTO
CREDITS

ABOUT
THE
AUTHOR

Jack Hanna has been around animals all his life. Director of the Columbus Zoo since 1978, he is a regular guest on "Good Morning America" and "Late Night with David Letterman," and has traveled in the past five years to India, Africa, South America, the Galápagos Islands, and China. He is also a Professional Fellow of the American Association of Zoological Parks and Aquariums. Jack currently lives in Dublin, Ohio, with his wife, Suzi, and his three daughters.

BOOK MARK

*The text of this book was composed in
the typefaces Weiss and
Trade Gothic Condensed Italic
by Folio Graphics Company, Inc.,
New York, New York*

*The color separations were produced
by Folio Graphics Company, Inc.,
New York, New York*

*The color inserts were printed
by Coral Graphics,
Plainview, New York*

*Text was printed on 60 lb. Finch Opaque
by Berryville Graphics,
Berryville, Virginia*

Endpaper map by Jackie Aher

*DESIGNED AND ILLUSTRATED
BY CAROL MALCOLM*